A Guide to THE BLESSING LIFE

40 Days of Scripture and Prayer

GERRIT DAWSON

IVP Books

An imprint of InterVarsity Press
Downers Grove, Illinois

InterVarsity Press
P.O. Box 1400, Downers Grove, IL 60515-1426
World Wide Web: www.ivpress.com
Email: email@ivpress.com

InterVarsity Press® is the book-publishing division of InterVarsity Christian Fellowship/USA®, a movement of students and faculty active on campus at hundreds of universities, colleges and schools of nursing in the United States of America, and a member movement of the International Fellowship of Evangelical Students. For information about local and regional activities, write Public Relations Dept., InterVarsity Christian Fellowship/USA, 6400 Schroeder Rd., P.O. Box 7895, Madison, WI 53707-7895, or visit the IVCF website at www.intervarsity.org.

Cover design: Cindy Kiple
Interior design: Beth Hagenberg
Images: © S-E-R-G-O/iStockphoto

ISBN 978-0-8308-3752-6 (print)
ISBN 978-0-8308-9584-7 (digital)

Printed in the United States of America ∞

Library of Congress Cataloging-in-Publication Data

Dawson, Gerrit Scott.
  A guide to the blessing life : 40 days of scripture and prayer / Gerrit Dawson.
     pages cm
  ISBN 978-0-8308-3752-6 (pbk. : alk. paper)
  1. God (Christianity)--Love--Prayers and devotions. 2. Love--Religious
aspects--Christianity--Prayers and devotions. 3. Spiritual
life--Christianity--Prayers and devotions. 4. Christian life--Prayers
and devotions. I. Title.
  BT140.D39 2013
  242'.2--dc23
                                                             2013014773

P	18	17	16	15	14	13	12	11	10	9	8	7	6	5	4	3	2	1
Y	28	27	26	25	24	23	22	21	20	19	18	17	16	15	14	13		

CONTENTS

INTRODUCTION

A blessing is not simply what you say before a meal or after someone sneezes. A blessing is not just having everything work out the way we want it. And blessing is certainly not defined by how cool the stuff is that comes to us. Of course, all those things are part of the true meaning of blessing. But they are merely ripples on the surface of the deep ocean of God's blessing to us—indeed to the whole world—in Christ Jesus.

Do you want to live in a way so rich that it could be described as a life of blessing? If those words tug at your heart even a little bit, then you know we have to go deeper. So we turn to God's Word.

Jesus' friend and disciple Peter began his second letter with a powerful blessing for his readers. He prayed, "May grace and peace be multiplied to you in the knowledge of God and of Jesus our Lord" (2 Peter 1:2). A life defined by ever-overflowing peace and grace would surely be a life of blessing. According to Peter, these qualities get multiplied in us through knowing Jesus. That makes sense. I believe that knowing Jesus is knowing the source of blessing himself.

Peter took it further: "His divine power has granted to us all things that pertain to life and godliness" (2 Peter 1:3). The deep life of blessing is already ours! We just have to learn how to realize it. Whatever we need for a life of blessing we already have through God's power. Peter goes on to say that this comes through "knowledge of him who called us to his own glory and excellence" (2 Peter 1:3). Once again, knowing Jesus is the key to the life of blessing. It's what steps us up into the glory and excellence of God. But how do we get to know him?

> *What would happen if every day for 40 days,*
>
> *1. I experienced the blessing of God's love more deeply?*
>
> *2. I blessed God for his love more passionately?*
>
> *3. I blessed others with his love more intentionally?*

Next, Peter got more specific: "He has granted to us his precious and very great promises, so that through them you may become partakers of the divine nature" (2 Peter 1:4). In God's Word are very great and precious promises. They point us to Jesus, the blessing of God wrapped in skin and bone. We get to know him as we listen to him through his Word. We come close to him as we ponder who he is and what he has done.

This is how it works. There are three simple but profound steps:

1. *We receive the blessing of "his very great and precious promises" through his Word.* We drink God's promises in as we read. We think about them. We take them in faith as belonging to us. We agree to let them shape our view of the world, our values and our actions. As we study we learn what God is up to in this world. We see how he's on a massive blessing project that extends to the farthest ends of the earth. In other words, we read his Word in order to get in step with God's blessing program. In so doing we become more and more joined to Jesus himself.

2. *We return the blessing to God.* Having received his great promises as a blessing to us, we bless God back, so to speak, by praising him for who he has shown himself to be and for all he has done to redeem the world. We lift up beyond ourselves and talk to God about himself. We speak aloud, we sing, we think, we write— we worship. We expend energy toward God.

This crucial activity is difficult for us, for blessing God is more than thanks. It involves really thinking about who he is, then making the effort to express his glory and grace back to him. We're not well-trained in blessing God. We may begin by being able to say only, "God, you're great!" But practice and rehearsal will take us farther quickly, especially as we use God's own Word as the source material for blessing him.

3. We reflect the blessing of God to others. We step into the flow of our blessing God by extending his blessing to those around us. Blessing is not meant to be kept to ourselves. And God's blessing is not lost by sharing it. In fact, the only way we can live the blessing life is to bless others. This may be through faithful prayer for them. Or perhaps through acts of kindness. Or through words of encouragement that build someone up. Best of all, when we have earned a hearing through our love and listening, we may be able to speak the specific promises of God to someone and lead him or her to knowing Christ more deeply.

I believe that engaging these three steps will enable us to know Jesus more and more in faith and trust. As we do, Peter has told us, we partake of Christ's very nature. Joined to him, we enter the life of blessing as we praise him in prayer and worship. That life then flourishes and grows as we share Christ with others in this weary and broken world.

How Does It Work?

Practicing forty days of blessing is an invitation to live these three steps intentionally. Here's how it works.

Give God fifteen minutes. Every morning for the next six weeks, set aside about a quarter-hour for engaging God's Word. Each day you'll be guided to passages through which you can discover the blessing God has to give to you and through you.

Receive the blessing. This study guide takes you to some of the all-time-great passages about God's blessing to us and leads you to consider how they apply to you.

Read passages that bless God. This guide will invite you to make prayers offered in return for God's love and mercy your own.

Read passages about blessing others. Through these Scriptures you will be invited to bless others amidst your daily activities.

Put what you've learned into action. A practical blessing step follows so that each day you can concentrate on a way specifically to live the blessing life.

Also, I invite you to take a few minutes each night to look back on the day and consider the blessing opportunities that came your way. Go back over the blessing-God verse from the morning and offer it to him as praise before you sleep. On the weekends, there will be suggestions for further review.

Now, of course you can do these forty days of blessing individually, but I believe the blessing life is most successfully entered through community. Along with regular worship in church, a weekly small group studying the biblical meaning of blessing can be the proving ground for your daily individual work.

I encourage you to stick with it. If you miss a day, don't quit. Just pick back up with the next day. If it seems difficult at first to focus, just keep at it day by day. You are building "blessing muscles" and that takes time. Give these fifteen minutes a day to focus on the blessing life and see where God takes you!

If you engage this experiment vigorously, at the end of forty days you will have blessed God and others more intentionally and consistently than ever before. That will change your life!

Week One

Receive the Blessing of God

> For God so loved the world, that he gave his only Son, that whoever believes in him should not perish but have eternal life. For God did not send his Son into the world to condemn the world, but in order that the world might be saved through him. (John 3:16-17)

How is God blessing his people in this passage? What is he promising? In what relationship or situation would you particularly desire this blessing to be active today? Finish this question: If this promise is true, then today . . .

Return the Blessing to God

> Bless the LORD, O my soul,
>   and all that is within me,
>   bless his holy name!
> Bless the LORD, O my soul,
>   and forget not all his benefits,
> who forgives all your iniquity,
>   who heals all your diseases,
> who redeems your life from the pit,
>   who crowns you with steadfast love and mercy,
> who satisfies you with good
>   so that your youth is renewed like the eagle's.
>   (Psalm 103:1-5)

Reflect the Blessing of God to Others

May the God of hope fill you with all joy and peace in believing, so that by the power of the Holy Spirit you may abound in hope. (Romans 15:13)

Pray this blessing on behalf of a particular family member or friend. Is there any special need you want to pray for? Consider how you might make contact and be a blessing in his or her life today. Would it be possible to share this verse in an email, text or card?

Practical Blessing

Smile! Be intentional today about smiling at others. It seems like a small thing, but smiles communicate favor and acceptance. Your smile, then, opens a window to the reality that you know the favor and acceptance of God and are willing to share it. Many of us are so intent on our tasks or so full of worry that we forget to smile. Give others the blessing of your shining countenance today.

....

Week One

Day 2: Monday Morning

Receive the Blessing of God

The LORD spoke to Moses, saying, "Speak to Aaron and his sons, saying, Thus you shall bless the people of Israel: you shall say to them,

The LORD bless you and keep you;
the LORD make his face to shine upon you and be
    gracious to you;
the LORD lift up his countenance upon you and give you
    peace.

"So shall they put my name upon the people of Israel, and
I will bless them." (Numbers 6:22-27)

Consider how this passage expresses the ways the Lord blesses
his people: If God's face is shining upon you, what does this mean?
If God is keeping you today, what does this mean? If God's name is
branded onto your heart and spirit, what does this mean?

Return the Blessing to God

O God, you are my God; earnestly I seek you;
    my soul thirsts for you;
my flesh faints for you,
    as in a dry and weary land where there is no water.
So I have looked upon you in the sanctuary,
    beholding your power and glory.
Because your steadfast love is better than life,
    my lips will praise you.
So I will bless you as long as I live;
    in your name I will lift up my hands. (Psalm 63:1-4)

Pray this blessing aloud at least three times. Try to attach your
heart and mind to the words as you pray. Feel free to elaborate on
the passage in your praise of God.

Reflect the Blessing of God to Others

I thank my God through Jesus Christ for all of you, because
your faith is proclaimed in all the world. (Romans 1:8)

Write a list of three to four people for whose faith you are particularly thankful. Hold each of them before the Lord. Pray this
verse over their lives and ask for God's strengthening and effec-
tiveness. Consider how you might send or speak this verse to that
person today.

Practical Blessing

Thank! Be intentional about thanking others today. Gratitude recognizes that what we receive has a source outside of ourselves. By being thanking people, we positively point others to the God from whom all blessings flow. We also communicate favor and create good will.

....

Week One

Day 3: Tuesday Morning

Receive the Blessing of God

> Jesus said to her, "Everyone who drinks of this water will be thirsty again, but whoever drinks of the water that I will give him will never be thirsty again. The water that I will give him will become in him a spring of water welling up to eternal life." (John 4:13-14)

> On the last day of the feast, the great day, Jesus stood up and cried out, "If anyone thirsts, let him come to me and drink. Whoever believes in me, as the Scripture has said, 'Out of his heart will flow rivers of living water.'" (John 7:37-38)

On Tuesdays we will be considering passages from John in which Jesus declares great things about himself. Today we are looking at how Jesus is living water. What kind of thirst does Jesus promise to satisfy? If living water were flowing freely through your life today, what do you imagine would happen? Will you in this moment drink of Jesus by faith, welcoming his presence in your heart, asking him to live in you from the inside out?

Return the Blessing to God

I say to the LORD, "You are my Lord;
    I have no good apart from you." . . .

I bless the LORD who gives me counsel;
    in the night also my heart instructs me.
I have set the LORD always before me;
    because he is at my right hand, I shall not be shaken. . . .

You make known to me the path of life;
    in your presence there is fullness of joy;
    at your right hand are pleasures forevermore.
        (Psalm 16:2, 7-8, 11)

Pray this blessing aloud at least three times. Try to attach your heart to the words. Then feel free to elaborate on the words in your praise and blessing of God.

Reflect the Blessing of God to Others

I will tell of your name to my brothers;
    in the midst of the congregation I will praise you.
        (Psalm 22:22)

Consider today who might be blessed by your speaking and praising of God. Is there an email you could write that includes the words, "Today, I am praising God for _____ and I just wanted you to know how good he has been in my life"? Be on the alert for an opportunity during a conversation to speak well of God before someone today.

Practical Blessing

Compliment! Say something nice to those in your life today. Point out something good they say or do. Give them the grace of acceptance. Bless them by speaking about what they've done that is good. God is good, and all human excellence partakes of him.

....

Week One

Day 4: Wednesday Morning

Receive the Blessing of God

For to us a child is born,
    to us a son is given;
and the government shall be upon his shoulder,
    and his name shall be called
Wonderful Counselor, Mighty God,
    Everlasting Father, Prince of Peace.
Of the increase of his government and of peace
    there will be no end,
on the throne of David and over his kingdom,
    to establish it and to uphold it
with justice and with righteousness
    from this time forth and forevermore.
The zeal of the LORD of hosts will do this. (Isaiah 9:6-7)

On Wednesdays during our forty days we will receive passages from the prophet Isaiah. Consider all God is promising us in this passage. What will the world be like when he reigns over all? Now consider, "Today I have a Wonderful Counselor with me. He speaks to me from his Word and by his Spirit in my heart. I belong to a Mighty God. He is my Father and considers me his beloved child." What peace is the Prince of Peace offering in the situations you will face?

Return the Blessing to God

I love the LORD, because he has heard
  my voice and my pleas for mercy.
Because he inclined his ear to me,
  therefore I will call on him as long as I live.
The snares of death encompassed me;
  the pangs of Sheol laid hold on me;
  I suffered distress and anguish.
Then I called on the name of the LORD:
  "O LORD, I pray, deliver my soul!"

Gracious is the LORD, and righteous;
  our God is merciful.
The LORD preserves the simple;
  when I was brought low, he saved me.
Return, O my soul, to your rest;
  for the LORD has dealt bountifully with you.
For you have delivered my soul from death,
  my eyes from tears,
  my feet from stumbling;
I will walk before the LORD
  in the land of the living. (Psalm 116:1-9)

Pray this blessing aloud at least three times. Try to attach your
heart to the words. Then feel free to elaborate on the words in your
praise and blessing of God.

Reflect the Blessing of God to Others

May God be gracious to us and bless us
  and make his face to shine upon us,
that your way may be known on earth,
  your saving power among all nations.

Let the peoples praise you, O God;
　　let all the peoples praise you!

Let the nations be glad and sing for joy,
　　for you judge the peoples with equity
　　and guide the nations upon earth.
Let the peoples praise you, O God;
　　let all the peoples praise you!

The earth has yielded its increase;
　　God, our God, shall bless us.
God shall bless us;
　　let all the ends of the earth fear him! (Psalm 67)

God's blessing project extends to the ends of the earth. The Lord desires to bring his saving power to bear among all nations. Pray for the church throughout the world. Pray for those who have never heard of Jesus. Pray for the missionaries your church supports. Hold up the news of world affairs in light of God's vision for blessing the world.

Practical Blessing

Notice! So often we hurry by without even seeing each other. Make an effort today to slow down and notice the people who are in your life. Notice them and give thanks. But notice also how it seems to be going with them. Is there care on their brow? Joy in their smile? Burden in their walk? Pay attention and make note.

....

Week One

Day 5: Thursday Morning

Receive the Blessing of God

Therefore, since we have been justified by faith, we have peace with God through our Lord Jesus Christ. Through him we have also obtained access by faith into this grace in which we stand, and we rejoice in hope of the glory of God. Not only that, but we rejoice in our sufferings, knowing that suffering produces endurance, and endurance produces character, and character produces hope, and hope does not put us to shame, because God's love has been poured into our hearts through the Holy Spirit who has been given to us. (Romans 5:1-5)

Name the two reasons for rejoicing specifically mentioned in this passage, and consider what is the source of that joy. What else does this passage say that God has given us? As you prepare for the day before you, in what circumstances will you especially want to remember that "God's love has been poured into our hearts"?

Return the Blessing to God

Blessed be the God and Father of our Lord Jesus Christ! According to his great mercy, he has caused us to be born again to a living hope through the resurrection of Jesus Christ from the dead, to an inheritance that is imperishable, undefiled, and unfading, kept in heaven for you, who by God's power are being guarded through faith for a salvation ready to be revealed in the last time. (1 Peter 1:3-5)

Praise God for this great salvation he has accomplished! Pray this passage aloud, attaching your hearts to the words. Then tell God about his salvation in Christ—elaborate on this passage to bless him for what he has done.

Reflect the Blessing of God to Others

"You have heard that it was said, 'You shall love your neighbor and hate your enemy.' But I say to you, Love your enemies and pray for those who persecute you, so that you may be sons of your Father who is in heaven. For he makes his sun rise on the evil and on the good, and sends rain on the just and on the unjust. For if you love those who love you, what reward do you have?" (Matthew 5:43-46)

While we were enemies, God reconciled us to himself in Christ. Now he asks us to pray for and love our enemies. Identify one to three people who might be on this list for you. There may be active hostility or simply years of barriers and ignoring of each other. Can you ask for God's will to be done in their life and for his love to be active in them? Is there anything for which you need to apologize? Is there any gesture of peace you might make?

Practical Blessing

Inquire! As you notice others, consider how to make inquiries about their well-being. Cross the divide of silence that exists between so many of us. Ask questions that help you connect to another person and show you care.

....

Week One

Day 6: Friday Morning

Receive the Blessing of God

"Behold, the days are coming, declares the LORD, when I will make a new covenant with the house of Israel and the house of Judah, not like the covenant that I made with their fathers on the day when I took them by the hand to bring them out of the land of Egypt, my covenant that they broke, though I was their husband, declares the LORD. For this is the covenant that I will make with the house of Israel after those days, declares the LORD: I will put my law within them, and I will write it on their hearts. And I will be their God, and they shall be my people. And no longer shall each one teach his neighbor and each his brother, saying, 'Know the LORD,' for they shall all know me, from the least of them to the greatest, declares the LORD. For I will forgive their iniquity, and I will remember their sin no more." (Jeremiah 31:31-34)

Every Friday we will read a passage from the Old Testament that reveals God's *big* purpose of salvation. From this Jeremiah passage, what changes in the way we view our lives if we realize that the Lord has bound himself to us as our saving, loving God? What changes in my day if I come awake to the reality that I belong to the claimed, redeemed, beloved people of God?

Return the Blessing to God

Blessed be the Lord,
    who daily bears us up;
    God is our salvation.
Our God is a God of salvation,
    and to GOD, the Lord, belong deliverances from death.
        (Psalm 68:19-20)

As you pray this blessing aloud at least three times, consider how the Lord has borne you up in day to day life. Consider how the Lord has delivered you from death and given you salvation. Go on to bless him for the reasons why you can join your voice to the words from Psalm 68.

Reflect the Blessing of God to Others

"Is not this the fast that I choose:
    to loose the bonds of wickedness,

to undo the straps of the yoke,
to let the oppressed go free,
 and to break every yoke?
Is it not to share your bread with the hungry
 and bring the homeless poor into your house;
when you see the naked, to cover him,
 and not to hide yourself from your own flesh?
Then shall your light break forth like the dawn,
 and your healing shall spring up speedily;
your righteousness shall go before you;
 the glory of the LORD shall be your rear guard. . . .
And your ancient ruins shall be rebuilt;
 you shall raise up the foundations of many generations;
you shall be called the repairer of the breach,
 the restorer of streets to dwell in." (Isaiah 58:6-8, 12)

The Lord's blessing of the world takes very concrete forms. In what ways are you being called to share bread with the hungry? To house the homeless? To rebuild lives and neighborhoods that are in ruins? What is your church doing in this regard? How might you get more connected with God's blessing project of the broken and needy?

> **Expand the Blessing**
>
> *"I will be your God and you will be my people" is the phrase of covenant communion we read from Genesis to Revelation. This is God's intention. This is why we are here. Blessing is communion in God who is love, which brings forth the fruit of love in our lives overflowing to others. Blessing is not first of all material prosperity, which may or may not occur. Rather, blessing is the fruitfulness of life lived in loving relation to God and others.*

Practical Blessing

Give something! Consider if this is the day to bring that stack of old blankets to the shelter, to drop off a coat for the poor or bring some cans of food to the food bank. Make your faith concrete today.

....

Week One

Day 7: Saturday Morning

Receive the Blessing of God

> For all have sinned and fall short of the glory of God, and are justified by his grace as a gift, through the redemption that is in Christ Jesus, whom God put forward as a propitiation by his blood, to be received by faith. This was to show God's righteousness, because in his divine forbearance he had passed over former sins. It was to show his righteousness at the present time, so that he might be just and the justifier of the one who has faith in Jesus. (Romans 3:23-26)

On Saturdays, we will be considering God's great promises from Romans. What's freeing about realizing that on our own we fall short of God's glory and will? Do you in this moment accept the gift of grace, the forgiveness of sins that comes through Jesus Christ? What will change in your day as you hold this grace in your mind and heart?

Return the Blessing to God

> How lovely is your dwelling place,
>> O Lord of hosts!
> My soul longs, yes, faints
>> for the courts of the Lord;

my heart and flesh sing for joy
  to the living God.

Even the sparrow finds a home,
  and the swallow a nest for herself,
  where she may lay her young,
at your altars, O Lord of hosts,
  my King and my God.

Blessed are those who dwell in your house,
  ever singing your praise!
Blessed are those whose strength is in you,
  in whose heart are the highways to Zion.
As they go through the Valley of Baca
  they make it a place of springs;
  the early rain also covers it with pools.
They go from strength to strength. . . .

For a day in your courts is better
  than a thousand elsewhere.
I would rather be a doorkeeper in the house of my God
  than dwell in the tents of wickedness. (Psalm 84:1-7, 10)

Pray this psalm aloud at least twice. As you do, consider how good and sweet it is to worship God in the company of others. Consider the joy of praising God in the midst of his people. Pray for the worship of your church that will occur tomorrow. Pray for the message your pastor is preparing. Prepare your heart in anticipation of being able to sing and pray God's praises together.

Reflect the Blessing of God to Others

Finally, all of you, have unity of mind, sympathy, brotherly love, a tender heart, and a humble mind. Do not repay evil for

evil or reviling for reviling, but on the contrary, bless, for to
this you were called, that you may obtain a blessing. For

> "Whoever desires to love life
>   and see good days,
> let him keep his tongue from evil
>   and his lips from speaking deceit;
> let him turn away from evil and do good;
>   let him seek peace and pursue it.
> For the eyes of the Lord are on the righteous,
>   and his ears are open to their prayer.
> But the face of the Lord is against those who do evil."
>   (1 Peter 3:8-12)

On the contrary, bless! Consider your usual reaction to sarcastic
remarks, slights or indifference. What would it look like to have a
tender heart toward those who hurt you? How can you prepare
words of blessing to have at the ready the next time you get
"slimed" by someone? How can you be an energy changer who
turns gossip and slights into affirmation and blessing?

Weekend Blessing

Take a few extra minutes to reflect on your first week of intentionally blessing God and others. Were you more aware of the
presence of God? Did opportunities to bless others increase?

Written Blessings

In these days of electronic communication, handwritten notes
have become rare. Yet when we put pen to paper, we actually give
a bit of ourselves to someone. We have literally touched that communication and expressed our thoughts through our hands. Consider to whom you might write a note of blessing today. Bless them
with a compliment. Bless them by writing out a prayer for them.

Bless them with words about our triune God of grace. Give it to the person or mail it today.

. . . .

Week Two

Day 8: Sunday Morning

Receive the Blessing of God

> Long ago, at many times and in many ways, God spoke to our fathers by the prophets, but in these last days he has spoken to us by his Son, whom he appointed the heir of all things, through whom also he created the world. He is the radiance of the glory of God and the exact imprint of his nature, and he upholds the universe by the word of his power. After making purification for sins, he sat down at the right hand of the Majesty on high, having become as much superior to angels as the name he has inherited is more excellent than theirs. (Hebrews 1:1-4)

How has God spoken to us in Jesus? What are three things about Jesus the Son of God that are taught us in this passage? What does it mean for you today that God has not gone silent for you, has not turned away from you, but instead speaks his love by offering you his Son?

Return the Blessing to God

> Oh come, let us sing to the LORD;
>   let us make a joyful noise to the rock of our salvation!
> Let us come into his presence with thanksgiving;
>   let us make a joyful noise to him with songs of praise!
> For the LORD is a great God,

and a great King above all gods.
In his hand are the depths of the earth;
    the heights of the mountains are his also.
The sea is his, for he made it,
    and his hands formed the dry land.

Oh come, let us worship and bow down;
    let us kneel before the LORD, our Maker!
For he is our God,
    and we are the people of his pasture,
and the sheep of his hand. (Psalm 95:1-7)

Pray this Psalm aloud in different levels of voice. Pray it in a normal voice, then pray it aloud with great enthusiasm. Consider singing it according to whatever tune comes to you. Bless the Lord as you describe his greatness through these words.

Reflect the Blessing of God to Others

Now may the God of peace who brought again from the dead our Lord Jesus, the great shepherd of the sheep, by the blood of the eternal covenant, equip you with everything good that you may do his will, working in us that which is pleasing in his sight, through Jesus Christ, to whom be glory forever and ever. Amen. (Hebrews 13:20-21)

Consider those you know who need strengthening to face life and enact God's will. Pray for specific equipping to suit their situation. Pray that God will work in them to make them a pleasure in his sight. Consider sending this verse to someone as you let them know you prayed.

Practical Blessing

Cultivate courtesy! Old-fashioned courtesy provides a way to honor another person, so it is a way of blessing. Through courtesy, we put ourselves second and defer to others. Make it a point today to open a door for someone, to offer to carry a load, to give up your seat or in any other way to speak and act graciously.

....

Week Two

Day 9: Monday Morning

Receive the Blessing of God

> And the angel said to her, "Do not be afraid, Mary, for you have found favor with God. And behold, you will conceive in your womb and bear a son, and you shall call his name Jesus. He will be great and will be called the Son of the Most High. And the Lord God will give to him the throne of his father David, and he will reign over the house of Jacob forever, and of his kingdom there will be no end."
>
> And Mary said to the angel, "How will this be, since I am a virgin?"
>
> And the angel answered her, "The Holy Spirit will come upon you, and the power of the Most High will overshadow you; therefore the child to be born will be called holy—the Son of God. And behold, your relative Elizabeth in her old age has also conceived a son, and this is the sixth month with her who was called barren. For nothing will be impossible with God." And Mary said, "Behold, I am the servant of the Lord; let it be to me according to your word." And the angel departed from her. (Luke 1:30-38)

What is God doing for the world in this passage? Mary receives the blessing of God by saying, "Behold, I am the servant of the Lord; let it be to me according to your word." This is the perfect response of faith. Consider how you can accept today the Lord's promises by praying, "Let it be to me according to your Word."

Return the Blessing to God

And Mary said,

"My soul magnifies the Lord,
    and my spirit rejoices in God my Savior,
for he has looked on the humble estate of his servant.
    For behold, from now on all generations will call me
        blessed;
for he who is mighty has done great things for me,
    and holy is his name.
And his mercy is for those who fear him
    from generation to generation.
He has shown strength with his arm;
    he has scattered the proud in the thoughts of their hearts;
he has brought down the mighty from their thrones
    and exalted those of humble estate;
he has filled the hungry with good things,
    and the rich he has sent away empty.
He has helped his servant Israel,
    in remembrance of his mercy,
as he spoke to our fathers,
    to Abraham and to his offspring forever." (Luke 1:46-55)

Can we join Mary in praising God for sending Jesus Christ into the world through her? As you bless God aloud through this prayer known as the Magnificat, feel along with Mary the wonder at what God is doing to save us and bless us.

Reflect the Blessing of God to Others

> Love is patient and kind; love does not envy or boast; it is not arrogant or rude. It does not insist on its own way; it is not irritable or resentful; it does not rejoice at wrongdoing, but rejoices with the truth. Love bears all things, believes all things, hopes all things, endures all things. Love never ends. (1 Corinthians 13:4-8)

Consider in prayer those two or three people with whom you have the most interaction in your life. How can you bless them specifically today by enacting the definition of love described in 1 Corinthians?

Practical Blessing

Touch! We connect to one another through physical contact. Of course, you have to consider what level of contact is appropriate with each person or situation. But be intentional today about touching an arm or shoulder of someone, offering a hug or even making sure your handshakes communicate personal warmth.

....

Week Two

Day 10: Tuesday Morning

Receive the Blessing of God

> Jesus said to them, "I am the bread of life; whoever comes to me shall not hunger, and whoever believes in me shall never thirst." (John 6:35)

> "Truly, truly, I say to you, whoever believes has eternal life. I am the bread of life. Your fathers ate the manna in the wilderness, and they died. This is the bread that comes down

from heaven, so that one may eat of it and not die. I am the living bread that came down from heaven. If anyone eats of this bread, he will live forever. And the bread that I will give for the life of the world is my flesh." (John 6:47-51)

Tuesday means great passages from the Gospel of John. What hunger does Jesus alone satisfy? What does his "bread" give to those who eat it? Consider how in giving us his flesh Jesus has held nothing back from us. In what "hungry" situations of your life might this be good news?

Return the Blessing to God

Blessed be the God and Father of our Lord Jesus Christ, who has blessed us in Christ with every spiritual blessing in the heavenly places, even as he chose us in him before the foundation of the world, that we should be holy and blameless before him. In love he predestined us for adoption as sons through Jesus Christ, according to the purpose of his will, to the praise of his glorious grace, with which he has blessed us in the Beloved. In him we have redemption through his blood, the forgiveness of our trespasses, according to the riches of his grace, which he lavished upon us, in all wisdom and insight making known to us the mystery of his will, according to his purpose, which he set forth in Christ as a plan for the fullness of time, to unite all things in him, things in heaven and things on earth. (Ephesians 1:3-10)

After you have read this passage aloud at least twice, make a list of at least five things God has done in Jesus Christ. Pray these mighty acts back to him in thanks and praise.

Reflect the Blessing of God to Others

But you are a chosen race, a royal priesthood, a holy nation, a people for his own possession, that you may proclaim the excellencies of him who called you out of darkness into his marvelous light. Once you were not a people, but now you are God's people; once you had not received mercy, but now you have received mercy.

Beloved, I urge you as sojourners and exiles to abstain from the passions of the flesh, which wage war against your soul. Keep your conduct among the Gentiles honorable, so that when they speak against you as evildoers, they may see your good deeds and glorify God on the day of visitation. (1 Peter 2:9-12)

Peter calls us to proclaim the excellencies of him who called us. Could you list three or four of God's excellencies? When today might you be able to share that list with someone? Can you bear witness that his salvation is real and true in your life? What conduct does Peter give us that will put the proof to our praises? Where is this applicable in your blessing life today?

Practical Blessing

Close your mouth! While we are called to proclaim the excellencies of our God, we are also called in some situations to say nothing—our silence can be a blessing. Be aware today of whether it would be best to save some comments or advice for another time.

....

Week Two

Day 11: Wednesday Morning

Receive the Blessing of God

It shall come to pass in the latter days
    that the mountain of the house of the LORD

shall be established as the highest of the mountains,
  and shall be lifted up above the hills;
and all the nations shall flow to it,
  and many peoples shall come, and say:
"Come, let us go up to the mountain of the LORD,
  to the house of the God of Jacob,
that he may teach us his ways
  and that we may walk in his paths."
For out of Zion shall go the law,
  and the word of the LORD from Jerusalem.
He shall judge between the nations,
  and shall decide disputes for many peoples;
and they shall beat their swords into plowshares,
  and their spears into pruning hooks;
nation shall not lift up sword against nation,
  neither shall they learn war anymore.

O house of Jacob,
  come, let us walk
  in the light of the LORD. (Isaiah 2:2-5)

Often we look at the mess of the world and despair that nothing will ever change. But God has a different plan! Describe several characteristics of the Lord's vision for his world from this passage in Isaiah. Hold this vision before several difficult areas in your city or world today. Claim this future hope as you enter your day.

Return the Blessing to God

Out of the depths I cry to you, O LORD!
  O Lord, hear my voice!
Let your ears be attentive
  to the voice of my pleas for mercy!

If you, O LORD, should mark iniquities,
   O LORD, who could stand?
But with you there is forgiveness,
   that you may be feared.

I wait for the LORD, my soul waits,
   and in his word I hope;
my soul waits for the LORD
   more than watchmen for the morning,
   more than watchmen for the morning.

O Israel, hope in the LORD!
   For with the Lord there is steadfast love,
   and with him is plentiful redemption.
And he will redeem Israel
   from all his iniquities. (Psalm 130)

Read this Psalm aloud at least twice. Describe to the Lord the "plentiful redemption" he has brought to pass in your life. Praise God for the fact that with him there is forgiveness.

Reflect the Blessing of God to Others

Bearing with one another and, if one has a complaint against another, forgiving each other; as the Lord has forgiven you, so you also must forgive. (Colossians 3:13)

With the Lord there is forgiveness and plentiful redemption. How does that affect the way we bear with others and forgive them? Is there any situation or area of your life where you are not showing mercy and grace to the same level as you have been given mercy and grace? What can you do to bless someone with forbearance and forgiveness today?

Practical Blessing

Give the benefit of the doubt! Often I am quick to leap to judgment.

I see bad intent where there is none. I suspect motives that are actually good. But the blessing life gives others the benefit of the doubt. We choose to assume a good motive and intent in others unless we are definitely proved wrong. With whom might you need to give more benefit of the doubt?

....

Week Two

Day 12: Thursday Morning

Receive the Blessing of God

> No temptation has overtaken you that is not common to man. God is faithful, and he will not let you be tempted beyond your ability, but with the temptation he will also provide the way of escape, that you may be able to endure it. (1 Corinthians 10:13)

What is God promising in this passage? In what situation of your life today do you especially need this promise to hold true?

Return the Blessing to God

> Therefore do not be ashamed of the testimony about our Lord, nor of me his prisoner, but share in suffering for the gospel by the power of God, who saved us and called us to a holy calling, not because of our works but because of his own purpose and grace, which he gave us in Christ Jesus before the ages began, and which now has been manifested through the appearing of our Savior Christ Jesus, who abolished death and brought life and immortality to light through the gospel, for which I was appointed a preacher and apostle and teacher. (2 Timothy 1:8-11)

Are there any ways you have been called to share in suffering for the gospel? Can you bless God in the midst of this suffering? Bless God for the fact that he gave you his purpose and grace before the ages began—it's all a total gift!

Reflect the Blessing of God to Others

For to this you have been called, because Christ also suffered for you, leaving you an example, so that you might follow in his steps. He committed no sin, neither was deceit found in his mouth. When he was reviled, he did not revile in return; when he suffered, he did not threaten, but continued entrusting himself to him who judges justly. He himself bore our sins in his body on the tree, that we might die to sin and live to righteousness. By his wounds you have been healed. For you were straying like sheep, but have now returned to the Shepherd and Overseer of your souls. (1 Peter 2:21-25)

With which people do you especially need the example and power of the way Jesus suffered? How might the way you endure difficult times be a blessing to others? Where are you called to cease complaining and start praising in order to lift up those around you?

Practical Blessing

Be patient! An old-fashioned word for patience is long-suffering. That means putting up with situations and people that are tedious, annoying or difficult. Patient people are not surprised by frustrating circumstances but anticipate them. The long-suffering person trusts the presence of God in the midst of trial and waits for his deliverance.

Week Two

Day 13: Friday Morning

Receive the Blessing of God

> I will sprinkle clean water on you, and you shall be clean
> from all your uncleannesses, and from all your idols I will
> cleanse you. And I will give you a new heart, and a new spirit
> I will put within you. And I will remove the heart of stone
> from your flesh and give you a heart of flesh. And I will put
> my Spirit within you, and cause you to walk in my statutes
> and be careful to obey my rules. You shall dwell in the land
> that I gave to your fathers, and you shall be my people, and I
> will be your God. And I will deliver you from all your un-
> cleannesses. (Ezekiel 36:25-29)

It's Friday, so we have a big vision passage from the Old Testament. What is God promising his people? Look back at last Friday's verse. What are two key similarities? How does God give us a
new heart?

Return the Blessing to God

> And the four living creatures, each of them with six wings,
> are full of eyes all around and within, and day and night they
> never cease to say,
>
> > "Holy, holy, holy, is the Lord God Almighty,
> > who was and is and is to come!"
>
> And whenever the living creatures give glory and honor and
> thanks to him who is seated on the throne, who lives forever
> and ever, the twenty-four elders fall down before him who is
> seated on the throne and worship him who lives forever and

ever. They cast their crowns before the throne, saying,

> "Worthy are you, our Lord and God,
>> to receive glory and honor and power,
> for you created all things,
>> and by your will they existed and were created."
>> (Revelation 4:8-11)

As you pray this passage aloud two or three times, consider that you are joining your voice to the voices of mighty heavenly beings. You are taking up the words to the songs of heaven. Bless God in union with these spiritual powers.

Reflect the Blessing of God to Others

> But be doers of the word, and not hearers only, deceiving yourselves. (James 1:22)

> If anyone thinks he is religious and does not bridle his tongue but deceives his heart, this person's religion is worthless. Religion that is pure and undefiled before God, the Father, is this: to visit orphans and widows in their affliction, and to keep oneself unstained from the world. (James 1:26-27)

What are some specific ways James says we prove that our religion is real? There are literal orphans and widows all around us. There are also many other kinds of lonely and vulnerable people. Who is God bringing to your mind? Who are you called to visit or call today?

Practical Blessing

Serve! Serving another person takes humility but is one of the most powerful ways to bless him or her. It could be washing the dishes (without being asked), fixing a toilet, giving a ride or just fetching a drink. Look for an opportunity to serve someone today.

Week Two

Day 14: Saturday Morning

Receive the Blessing of God

> For while we were still weak, at the right time Christ died for
> the ungodly. For one will scarcely die for a righteous person—
> though perhaps for a good person one would dare even to
> die—but God shows his love for us in that while we were still
> sinners, Christ died for us. Since, therefore, we have now
> been justified by his blood, much more shall we be saved by
> him from the wrath of God. For if while we were enemies we
> were reconciled to God by the death of his Son, much more,
> now that we are reconciled, shall we be saved by his life.
> More than that, we also rejoice in God through our Lord
> Jesus Christ, through whom we have now received reconcili-
> ation. (Romans 5:6-11)

Saturday means receiving God's mighty blessings found in
Romans. Look again at this passage. What was our status when
Christ died for us? If that's true, then what have we done to earn
such a salvation? If God loves us even when we are at our worst,
what energy does that give us in facing the world today? What is
the basis for having joy in this life?

Return the Blessing to God

> It is good to give thanks to the LORD,
>   to sing praises to your name, O Most High;
> to declare your steadfast love in the morning,
>   and your faithfulness by night,

to the music of the lute and the harp,
  to the melody of the lyre.
For you, O LORD, have made me glad by your work;
  at the works of your hands I sing for joy.

How great are your works, O LORD!
  Your thoughts are very deep! (Psalm 92:1-5)

Pray this Psalm in response to the news of Romans 5. Declare to the Lord his steadfast love. Reflect back to him his faithfulness through the night. Consider singing the words to whatever tune comes to you.

Reflect the Blessing of God to Others

Flee from sexual immorality. Every other sin a person commits is outside the body, but the sexually immoral person sins against his own body. Or do you not know that your body is a temple of the Holy Spirit within you, whom you have from God? You are not your own, for you were bought with a price. So glorify God in your body. (1 Corinthians 6:18-20)

Having considered how great is our salvation, we see that in saving us, God also claims us. Consider whether you can accept this claim that "you are not your own, for you were bought with a price." Today especially consider if there is any sexual sin—in thought, word or deed—that you must release to the Lord.

Weekend Blessing

Walk your neighborhood! Often we drive in and drive out of our homes and never notice our street or our neighbors. Take a walk today in your neighborhood. Pray for your neighbors as you pass their homes. Speak to anyone you see. Notice your environs and give thanks.

Also, you've just finished your second week! Review your awareness of God's blessing presence in your life. Consider in what ways you have blessed others this week. Is there any blessing work left over from the last week that you can take care of today?

....

Week Three

Day 15: Sunday Morning

Receive the Blessing of God

> The saying is trustworthy and deserving of full acceptance, that Christ Jesus came into the world to save sinners, of whom I am the foremost. But I received mercy for this reason, that in me, as the foremost, Jesus Christ might display his perfect patience as an example to those who were to believe in him for eternal life. (1 Timothy 1:15-16)

Can you relate to Paul's saying that he is the foremost of sinners? There really is no competition for most sinful. The fact is that we can own our sin to the horrible depths and then hear the trustworthy news: Christ came to save sinners. He came to save us. Is there an area of guilt in your life where you need to accept that news today? Would you be willing to hold in your mind, for this entire day, the thought "I fully accept that Christ Jesus came to save me. Knowing full well who I am, he has saved this sinner entirely."

Return the Blessing to God

> Oh sing to the LORD a new song;
> sing to the LORD, all the earth!
> Sing to the LORD, bless his name;
> tell of his salvation from day to day.

Declare his glory among the nations,
his marvelous works among all the peoples!
For great is the LORD, and greatly to be praised;
he is to be feared above all gods.
For all the gods of the peoples are worthless idols,
but the LORD made the heavens.
Splendor and majesty are before him;
strength and beauty are in his sanctuary.

Ascribe to the LORD, O families of the peoples,
ascribe to the LORD glory and strength!
Ascribe to the LORD the glory due his name;
bring an offering, and come into his courts!
Worship the LORD in the splendor of holiness;
tremble before him, all the earth! (Psalm 96:1-9)

To "ascribe" means to credit a quality to someone. Today we join the author of Psalm 96 as we ascribe glory to the Lord. We credit God aloud for his mighty deeds and his kingship. Attach your heart, the heart saved by grace, to your praise. Bless the Lord for his faithfulness to you in Christ Jesus.

Reflect the Blessing of God to Others

I give thanks to my God always for you because of the grace of God that was given you in Christ Jesus, that in every way you were enriched in him in all speech and all knowledge— even as the testimony about Christ was confirmed among you—so that you are not lacking in any gift, as you wait for the revealing of our Lord Jesus Christ, who will sustain you to the end, guiltless in the day of our Lord Jesus Christ. God is faithful, by whom you were called into the fellowship of his Son, Jesus Christ our Lord. (1 Corinthians 1:4-9)

For whose faith do you especially give thanks? Who are the people in your daily life who seem rich with knowledge of Christ and words about him? Bless God for them today. Pray God's faithfulness over their lives. Will you email or write at least one of them today, blessing these people of great faith with the encouragement that "God will sustain you to the end" for "God is faithful"?

Practical Blessing

Appreciate! Let someone know how thankful you are for him or her. Say it specifically: "I'm so thankful for you. I thank God that he gave me you to know." Do it today!

....

Week Three

Day 16: Monday Morning

Receive the Blessing of God

But the angel said to him, "Do not be afraid, Zechariah, for your prayer has been heard, and your wife Elizabeth will bear you a son, and you shall call his name John. And you will have joy and gladness, and many will rejoice at his birth, for he will be great before the Lord. And he must not drink wine or strong drink, and he will be filled with the Holy Spirit, even from his mother's womb. And he will turn many of the children of Israel to the Lord their God, and he will go before him in the spirit and power of Elijah, to turn the hearts of the fathers to the children, and the disobedient to the wisdom of the just, to make ready for the Lord a people prepared." (Luke 1:13-17)

Zechariah was an elderly priest in Jerusalem. His wife Elizabeth was barren. When Zechariah was offering prayer and incense in the temple, an angel appeared to him. The angel told Zechariah that his wife would give birth to a son named John who would be the forerunner of the Christ. Can you receive the news today that God has a plan of salvation for this broken, weary world? Can you receive from this story the fact that you have a share in this salvation and a privileged calling to share among others the good news of Jesus?

Return the Blessing to God

And his father Zechariah was filled with the Holy Spirit and prophesied, saying,

"Blessed be the Lord God of Israel,
for he has visited and redeemed his people
and has raised up a horn of salvation for us
in the house of his servant David,
as he spoke by the mouth of his holy prophets from of old,
that we should be saved from our enemies
and from the hand of all who hate us;
to show the mercy promised to our fathers
and to remember his holy covenant,
the oath that he swore to our father Abraham, to grant us
that we, being delivered from the hand of our enemies,
might serve him without fear,
in holiness and righteousness before him all our days."
(Luke 1:67-75)

Join Zechariah in blessing God for the salvation he has raised up for us in Jesus Christ. Rejoice that the coming of Jesus was not just "out of the blue." For centuries it had been prophesied about and yearned for. Praise with Zechariah's father-joy as he realizes his boy John will give knowledge to people of God's forgiveness and tender mercy.

Reflect the Blessing of God to Others

> Now the time came for Elizabeth to give birth, and she bore a son. And her neighbors and relatives heard that the Lord had shown great mercy to her, and they rejoiced with her. And on the eighth day they came to circumcise the child. And they would have called him Zechariah after his father, but his mother answered, "No; he shall be called John." And they said to her, "None of your relatives is called by this name." And they made signs to his father, inquiring what he wanted him to be called. And he asked for a writing tablet and wrote, "His name is John." And they all wondered. And immediately his mouth was opened and his tongue loosed, and he spoke, blessing God. And fear came on all their neighbors. And all these things were talked about through all the hill country of Judea, and all who heard them laid them up in their hearts, saying, "What then will this child be?" For the hand of the Lord was with him. (Luke 1:57-66)

When Zechariah first heard the angel's news, he did not believe. As a result, he could not speak for nine months. But when the time came for his son to be named, Zechariah obeyed the angel's command to name him John. His obedience led to his speech being restored, and immediately he blessed God. This had a huge effect on others—this along with their joy for Elizabeth, who credited God for ending her barrenness.

Today, consider how your obedience to God and your public blessing of his goodness will affect others. Is there an area of your life where you have been facing a difficult choice of faithfulness?

Consider today how making the right choice will end up blessing others, even some you cannot see now.

Practical Blessing

Do the right thing! We serve the blessing God. We reflect his character when we live and act in accord with his Word. Others are blessed as over time we live consistently, honestly, kindly, diligently, faithfully. Be mindful of your choices today, and bless the world by doing the right thing.

....

Week Three

Day 17: Tuesday Morning

Receive the Blessing of God

> Again Jesus spoke to them, saying, "I am the light of the world. Whoever follows me will not walk in darkness, but will have the light of life." (John 8:12)

> So Jesus said to the Jews who had believed in him, "If you abide in my word, you are truly my disciples, and you will know the truth, and the truth will set you free." (John 8:31-32)

> Jesus said to him, "I am the way, and the truth, and the life. No one comes to the Father except through me." (John 14:6)

> Jesus said to them, "Truly, truly, I say to you, before Abraham was, I am." (John 8:58)

On Tuesdays we consider Jesus' declarations about himself in the Gospel of John. What is like to have "the light of life" amidst the darkness of this world? What is it like to know "the truth" amidst the lies and deceptions of this world? What difference does it make to be following the path to the Father rather than wandering on paths of our own devising? Can you receive the news that in giving us Jesus, his Father has given us light, truth and the way of life?

Return the Blessing to God

> Now to him who is able to keep you from stumbling and to present you blameless before the presence of his glory with great joy, to the only God, our Savior, through Jesus Christ our Lord, be glory, majesty, dominion, and authority, before all time and now and forever. Amen. (Jude 24-25)

As you pray Jude's benediction aloud several times, bless God that he has undertaken to join you to Jesus by his Spirit. This means he will lead you out of darkness in his light, out of error into his truth, out of the wilderness along his way. Bless the triune God in anticipation of the great moment when Jesus himself presents you blameless by his righteousness before the throne of God in great joy.

Reflect the Blessing of God to Others

> My mouth will tell of your righteous acts,
>> of your deeds of salvation all the day,
>>> for their number is past my knowledge.
> With the mighty deeds of the LORD God I will come;
>> I will remind them of your righteousness, yours alone.
>
> O God, from my youth you have taught me,
>> and I still proclaim your wondrous deeds.
> So even to old age and gray hairs,
>> O God, do not forsake me,

until I proclaim your might to another generation,
    your power to all those to come. (Psalm 71:15-18)

This morning we have reflected on how God has worked a
mighty act in our lives: he has brought us to himself in Jesus. List
two or three ways you have experienced the mighty deeds of the
triune God in your life. Now consider how you can join the psalmist
in letting your mouth tell of God's acts. How are you helping the
next generation to know the blessing of God? To whom are you
called to proclaim God's wondrous deeds in your life? Will you do
that today by an email, a phone call, a card or a conversation?

Practical Blessing

Drive to bless! Don't leave your faith outside your car. Drive in a
way that is gracious. Bless, don't curse, those other drivers. Give
way. Give room. Give grace on the road today.

....

Week Three

Day 18: Wednesday Morning

Receive the Blessing of God

There shall come forth a shoot from the stump of Jesse,
    and a branch from his roots shall bear fruit.
And the Spirit of the LORD shall rest upon him,
    the Spirit of wisdom and understanding,
    the Spirit of counsel and might,
    the Spirit of knowledge and the fear of the LORD.
And his delight shall be in the fear of the LORD.
He shall not judge by what his eyes see,
    or decide disputes by what his ears hear,

but with righteousness he shall judge the poor,
and decide with equity for the meek of the earth. . . .

The wolf shall dwell with the lamb,
     and the leopard shall lie down with the young goat. . . .
They shall not hurt or destroy
     in all my holy mountain;
for the earth shall be full of the knowledge of the LORD
     as the waters cover the sea.

     In that day the root of Jesse, who shall stand as a signal for
the peoples—of him shall the nations inquire, and his resting
place shall be glorious. (Isaiah 11:1-10)

Consider the future promised by God through "the shoot of
Jesse." Jesse was the father of David, Israel's great shepherd-king.
In Scripture's prophecies, the Messiah would be an offspring of
David, the true king who would reign over all. Look back over
these verses and list several characteristics of life when this king
fully reigns. We believe that Jesus is the true son of David, the
Messiah who came to us first to suffer and who will come again to
reign. What difference does it make as you start your day to know
Jesus' vision for this world?

Return the Blessing to God

For you formed my inward parts;
     you knitted me together in my mother's womb.
I praise you, for I am fearfully and wonderfully made.
Wonderful are your works;
     my soul knows it very well.
My frame was not hidden from you,
when I was being made in secret,
     intricately woven in the depths of the earth.

Your eyes saw my unformed substance;
in your book were written, every one of them,
    the days that were formed for me,
    when as yet there was none of them.

How precious to me are your thoughts, O God!
    How vast is the sum of them!
If I would count them, they are more than the sand.
    I awake, and I am still with you. (Psalm 139:13-18)

As you bless God aloud through this psalm, give thanks that God has made you as a unique, beloved child. Consider what it means that God's thoughts are always turned toward you, his dear little one, so that even when you return to consciousness from sleep, you find that he is there with you, that he has been there and always will be.

Reflect the Blessing of God to Others

And Jesus came and said to them, "All authority in heaven and on earth has been given to me. Go therefore and make disciples of all nations, baptizing them in the name of the Father and of the Son and of the Holy Spirit, teaching them to observe all that I have commanded you. And behold, I am with you always, to the end of the age." (Matthew 28:18-20)

Another way to translate Jesus' words is "As you are going, make disciples . . . " Every day we are going into our world, into our spheres of influence, into our regular relationships. Consider who you will meet this day. Pray for an opportunity to mention your Savior and for a way to show his love concretely.

Practical Blessing

See the whole field! Every part of your life is your mission field. We live the blessing life right where we work, play, eat, serve and interact. Open your eyes to the whole of life as a blessing field.

....

Week Three

Day 19: Thursday Morning

Receive the Blessing of God

> But when the goodness and loving kindness of God our Savior appeared, he saved us, not because of works done by us in righteousness, but according to his own mercy, by the washing of regeneration and renewal of the Holy Spirit, whom he poured out on us richly through Jesus Christ our Savior, so that being justified by his grace we might become heirs according to the hope of eternal life. (Titus 3:4-7)

God has saved us according to his mercy, not our deserving. Can you receive the news today that our triune God is full of "goodness and loving kindness"? Can you believe that he made this love appear when he entered the world in Jesus who saves us by his cross and resurrection? Will you receive his Spirit whom he longs to pour into your life? What difference will it make today to know that as you leave your home and enter the world, you walk about as "an heir of eternal life"?

Return the Blessing to God

> May you be strengthened with all power, according to his glorious might, for all endurance and patience with joy, giving thanks to the Father, who has qualified you to share in the inheritance of the saints in light. He has delivered us from the domain of darkness and transferred us to the kingdom of

his beloved Son, in whom we have redemption, the forgiveness of sins.

He is the image of the invisible God, the firstborn of all
creation. For by him all things were created, in heaven and on
earth, visible and invisible, whether thrones or dominions or
rulers or authorities—all things were created through him
and for him. And he is before all things, and in him all things
hold together. And he is the head of the body, the church. He
is the beginning, the firstborn from the dead, that in everything he might be preeminent. For in him all the fullness of
God was pleased to dwell, and through him to reconcile to
himself all things, whether on earth or in heaven, making
peace by the blood of his cross. (Colossians 1:11-23)

Give thanks to the Father who has qualified you for eternal life
through Christ. Give thanks that he has transferred you from the
domain of darkness to the kingdom of his beloved Son. Bless his
Son Jesus by praying aloud the descriptions of him in this passage.

Reflect the Blessing of God to Others

Remind them to be submissive to rulers and authorities, to be
obedient, to be ready for every good work, to speak evil of no
one, to avoid quarreling, to be gentle, and to show perfect
courtesy toward all people. For we ourselves were once
foolish, disobedient, led astray, slaves to various passions and
pleasures, passing our days in malice and envy, hated by
others and hating one another. (Titus 3:1-3)

As those who live in KBS today (the kingdom of the beloved
Son), we live by the code of conduct of our king. Prepare yourself
to show courtesy, especially in areas you'd be tempted to be rude.
Prepare yourself to speak well of others rather than evil, to avoid

quarreling and to seek peace. Recognize the temptation in a passion for gossip, anger and envy. Replace that passion with your desire to live as a son or daughter of the king.

Practical Blessing

Walk away! Sometimes we just have to leave a conversation if we know it's heading down the path of gossip or criticism. Don't get sucked into the downward whirlpool of cutting remarks. Bless by walking away.

Week Three

Day 20: Friday Morning

Receive the Blessing of God

"They shall not defile themselves anymore with their idols and their detestable things, or with any of their transgressions. But I will save them from all the backsliding in which they have sinned, and will cleanse them; and they shall be my people, and I will be their God.

"My servant David shall be king over them, and they shall all have one shepherd. They shall walk in my rules and be careful to obey my statutes. They shall dwell in the land that I gave to my servant Jacob, where your fathers lived. They and their children and their children's children shall dwell there forever, and David my servant shall be their prince forever. I will make a covenant of peace with them. It shall be an everlasting covenant with them. And I will set them in their land and multiply them, and will set my sanctuary in their midst forevermore. My dwelling place shall be with

them, and I will be their God, and they shall be my people.
Then the nations will know that I am the LORD who sanctifies
Israel, when my sanctuary is in their midst forevermore."
(Ezekiel 37:23-28)

Today we have another of the big vision passages from the Old
Testament. What does the Lord promise he will change in his
people? What is his ultimate goal in this passage? Jesus has established the new covenant in his blood—that is, in his faithfulness to
his Father even unto death. Joined to him we enter God's desire for
fellowship in which he is our God and we are his people. Will you
walk in that fellowship today?

Return the Blessing to God

And I saw what appeared to be a sea of glass mingled with
fire—and also those who had conquered the beast and its
image and the number of its name, standing beside the sea of
glass with harps of God in their hands. And they sing the song
of Moses, the servant of God, and the song of the Lamb, saying,

> "Great and amazing are your deeds,
>   O Lord God the Almighty!
> Just and true are your ways,
>   O King of the nations!
> Who will not fear, O Lord,
>   and glorify your name?
> For you alone are holy.
>   All nations will come
>   and worship you,
> for your righteous acts have been revealed."
>   (Revelation 15:2-4)

In this visionary passage we behold the faithful saints praising

God for his great deeds. Join your voice with these saints in heaven as you glorify God through their words.

Reflect the Blessing of God to Others

> Let brotherly love continue. Do not neglect to show hospitality to strangers, for thereby some have entertained angels unawares. Remember those who are in prison, as though in prison with them, and those who are mistreated, since you also are in the body. Let marriage be held in honor among all, and let the marriage bed be undefiled, for God will judge the sexually immoral and adulterous. Keep your life free from love of money, and be content with what you have, for he has said, "I will never leave you nor forsake you." (Hebrews 13:1-5)

The blessing life requires intentionality. We have to look for others to bless whom we might normally overlook. We have to hold true in the relationships we've been given. We have to want what we have more than striving to have what we want. In what specific ways does this passage speak to you today?

Practical Blessing

Park far! Consider leaving that close parking place for someone else. Take the farther spot and bless and pray as you walk in.

....

Week Three

Day 21: Saturday Morning

Receive the Blessing of God

> But the free gift is not like the trespass. For if many died through one man's trespass, much more have the grace of God

and the free gift by the grace of that one man Jesus Christ abounded for many. And the free gift is not like the result of that one man's sin. For the judgment following one trespass brought condemnation, but the free gift following many trespasses brought justification. For if, because of one man's trespass, death reigned through that one man, much more will those who receive the abundance of grace and the free gift of righteousness reign in life through the one man Jesus Christ.

Therefore, as one trespass led to condemnation for all men, so one act of righteousness leads to justification and life for all men. For as by the one man's disobedience the many were made sinners, so by the one man's obedience the many will be made righteous. Now the law came in to increase the trespass, but where sin increased, grace abounded all the more. (Romans 5:15-20)

On Saturdays we are considering the magnificent descriptions of salvation from the book of Romans. Consider the result of Adam's sin for the whole human race. Consider how Jesus is the new Adam, who obeyed where Adam disobeyed, who stood tall in faithfulness where Adam fell. What comes to us as we are joined to this new Adam?

Return the Blessing to God

Oh the depth of the riches and wisdom and knowledge of God! How unsearchable are his judgments and how inscrutable his ways!

"For who has known the mind of the Lord,
or who had been his counselor?"
"Or who has given a gift to him
that he might be repaid?"

For from him and through him and to him are all things. To him be glory forever. Amen. (Romans 11:33-36)

After spending eleven chapters describing the great salvation God has created for us in Jesus Christ, Paul just breaks into praise. Join him as you pray aloud this great passage to bless the triune God of grace.

Reflect the Blessing of God to Others

Therefore, having put away falsehood, let each one of you speak the truth with his neighbor, for we are members one of another. Be angry and do not sin; do not let the sun go down on your anger, and give no opportunity to the devil. Let the thief no longer steal, but rather let him labor, doing honest work with his own hands, so that he may have something to share with anyone in need. Let no corrupting talk come out of your mouths, but only such as is good for building up, as fits the occasion, that it may give grace to those who hear. And do not grieve the Holy Spirit of God, by whom you were sealed for the day of redemption. Let all bitterness and wrath and anger and clamor and slander be put away from you, along with all malice. Be kind to one another, tenderhearted, forgiving one another, as God in Christ forgave you. (Ephesians 4:25-32)

Weekend Blessing

We bless with our mouths. This passage sends us to consider where corrupting speech has come from us. Ask God to show you ways you have used your mouth to harm not bless. Take five full minutes to consider:

- lies or omissions of truth
- rash and angry rants, holding on to anger
- judgmental words, bitter feelings nurtured, slander

Confess and receive his forgiveness. Now consider how today you can use speech to build up another. Consider whom you need to forgive. Consider how you need to soften your heart in order to give the blessing of kindness. Is there anyone to whom you need to apologize? Write a specific plan for reversing your use of speech and ask the Spirit for power to enact it.

> **Expand the Blessing**
>
> *No more let sins or sorrows grow!*
> *Nor thorns infest the ground.*
> *He comes to make his blessings flow,*
> *Far as the curse is found,*
> *Far as the curse is found,*
> *Far as, far as the curse is found.*
>
> Isaac Watts, "Joy to the World" (see Psalm 96)

Week Four

Day 22: Sunday Morning

Receive the Blessing of God

Then I saw a new heaven and a new earth, for the first heaven and the first earth had passed away, and the sea was no more. And I saw the holy city, the new Jerusalem, coming down out of heaven from God, prepared as a bride adorned for her husband. And I heard a loud voice from the throne saying, "Behold, the dwelling place of God is with man. He will dwell with them, and they will be his people, and God himself will be with them as their God. He will wipe away every tear from their eyes, and death shall be no more, neither shall there be mourning nor crying nor pain anymore, for the former things have passed away."

And he who was seated on the throne said, "Behold, I am making all things new." (Revelation 21:1-5)

What connections do you see between this passage and the "big vision" passages we have been reading from the Old Testament prophets on Fridays? What hope does this picture of the future give you for today? What does this passage say to our grief, our illnesses and our anxiety? Could you spend a day thinking and acting as if this passage brought us the absolute truth about the future?

Return the Blessing to God

Oh sing to the LORD a new song,
    for he has done marvelous things!
His right hand and his holy arm
    have worked salvation for him.
The LORD has made known his salvation;
    he has revealed his righteousness in the sight of the nations.
He has remembered his steadfast love and faithfulness
    to the house of Israel.
All the ends of the earth have seen
    the salvation of our God.

Make a joyful noise to the LORD, all the earth;
    break forth into joyous song and sing praises!
Sing praises to the LORD with the lyre,
    with the lyre and the sound of melody!
With trumpets and the sound of the horn
    make a joyful noise before the King, the LORD!

Let the sea roar, and all that fills it;

the world and those who dwell in it!
Let the rivers clap their hands;
    let the hills sing for joy together
before the LORD, for he comes
    to judge the earth.
He will judge the world with righteousness,
    and the peoples with equity. (Psalm 98)

Recalling the vision of the new heavens and the new earth from Revelation 21, bless the Lord through praying or singing this psalm aloud.

Reflect the Blessing of God to Others

When they had finished breakfast, Jesus said to Simon Peter, "Simon, son of John, do you love me more than these?" He said to him, "Yes, Lord; you know that I love you." He said to him, "Feed my lambs." He said to him a second time, "Simon, son of John, do you love me?" He said to him, "Yes, Lord; you know that I love you." He said to him, "Tend my sheep." He said to him the third time, "Simon, son of John, do you love me?" Peter was grieved because he said to him the third time, "Do you love me?" and he said to him, "Lord, you know everything; you know that I love you." Jesus said to him, "Feed my sheep." (John 21:15-17)

Jesus linked Peter's love for him to Jesus' mission for Peter. We show God our love by loving his little lambs. As you prepare for worship and church this morning, which sheep do you feel called to tend? How will you do it?

Practical Blessing

Bless through time-keeping, part one: Be on time! We honor one another when we keep our time commitments. Arriving on time communicates, "You matter." Arriving on time at church shows respect for the worship leaders and blesses others as you help get the party started.

....

Week Four

Day 23: Monday Morning

Receive the Blessing of God

> And in the same region there were shepherds out in the field, keeping watch over their flock by night. And an angel of the Lord appeared to them, and the glory of the Lord shone around them, and they were filled with great fear. And the angel said to them, "Fear not, for behold, I bring you good news of great joy that will be for all the people. For unto you is born this day in the city of David a Savior, who is Christ the Lord. And this will be a sign for you: you will find a baby wrapped in swaddling cloths and lying in a manger." (Luke 2:8-12)

We continue our Monday look at Luke's account of Jesus' coming to us. Today we read the words of the herald angels. What is the promise of God to the world in this passage? How does this passage speak to your fears in life? Will you receive this angel song in your heart?

Return the Blessing to God

> And suddenly there was with the angel a multitude of the
>   heavenly host praising God and saying,
>
> "Glory to God in the highest,
>   and on earth peace among those with whom he
>   is pleased!"

When the angels went away from them into heaven, the shepherds said to one another, "Let us go over to Bethlehem and see this thing that has happened, which the Lord has made known to us." And they went with haste and found Mary and Joseph, and the baby lying in a manger. And when they saw it, they made known the saying that had been told them concerning this child. And all who heard it wondered at what the shepherds told them. But Mary treasured up all these things, pondering them in her heart. And the shepherds returned, glorifying and praising God for all they had heard and seen, as it had been told them. (Luke 2:13-20)

This morning, join your voice to the angels who glorified God for the birth of Jesus and his plan of salvation. Consider singing a Christmas hymn you know by heart, such as "Hark the Herald Angels" or "Joy to the World."

Reflect the Blessing of God to Others

I do not cease to give thanks for you, remembering you in my prayers, that the God of our Lord Jesus Christ, the Father of glory, may give you a spirit of wisdom and of revelation in the knowledge of him, having the eyes of your hearts enlightened, that you may know what is the hope to which he has called you. (Ephesians 1:16-18)

With Christmas joy from the passages above, for whom do you give particular thanks? Pray specifically that God would give these dear ones a spirit of truly knowing him more and more, that they would be filled with hope. Once again, considering sending this verse to the persons for whom you prayed.

Practical Blessing

Bless through time-keeping, part two: Arrive early! Showing up on time honors people. Showing up a few minutes early opens the door for blessing opportunities. Arrive early enough for conversation. Being early gives you time to notice, to ask, to share, to find openings for sharing the love of Christ and his gospel.

....

Week Four

Day 24: Tuesday Morning

Receive the Blessing of God

> So Jesus again said to them, "Truly, truly, I say to you, I am the door of the sheep. All who came before me are thieves and robbers, but the sheep did not listen to them. I am the door. If anyone enters by me, he will be saved and will go in and out and find pasture. The thief comes only to steal and kill and destroy. I came that they may have life and have it abundantly. I am the good shepherd. The good shepherd lays down his life for the sheep. . . . I am the good shepherd. I know my own and my own know me, just as the Father knows me and I know the Father; and I lay down my life for the sheep. . . .
>
> "My sheep hear my voice, and I know them, and they follow me. I give them eternal life, and they will never perish, and no one will snatch them out of my hand. My Father, who has given them to me, is greater than all, and no one is able to snatch them out of the Father's hand. I and the Father are one." (John 10:7-11, 14, 27-30)

Consider the wonder that you know the voice of the shepherd. When you read his Word, your heart is stirred—that's the shepherd's voice speaking through his Spirit within you! Consider that he knows you by name and loves you intimately. Consider that no one can snatch you from the Father's hand. What difference does that knowledge make in your day?

Return the Blessing to God

Blessed be the God and Father of our Lord Jesus Christ, the Father of mercies and God of all comfort, who comforts us in all our affliction, so that we may be able to comfort those who are in any affliction, with the comfort with which we ourselves are comforted by God. (2 Corinthians 1:3-4)

Bless the God and Father of our Lord Jesus for the comfort he gives you. Bless him for the assurance you received by reading the passage from John 10. Bless him for always showing up in the midst of difficult times. And consider that he has given you such comfort with a vision for you to comfort others with his truth.

Reflect the Blessing of God to Others

And we urge you, brothers, admonish the idle, encourage the fainthearted, help the weak, be patient with them all. See that no one repays anyone evil for evil, but always seek to do good to one another and to everyone. Rejoice always, pray without ceasing, give thanks in all circumstances; for this is the will of God in Christ Jesus for you. Do not quench the Spirit. Do not despise prophecies, but test everything; hold fast what is good.

Abstain from every form of evil.

Now may the God of peace himself sanctify you completely, and may your whole spirit and soul and body be kept blameless at the coming of our Lord Jesus Christ. He who calls you is faithful; he will surely do it. (1 Thessalonians 5:14-24)

The blessing life involves specific ways of acting in harmony with the love of Jesus Christ toward others. Read this passage through at least twice. Listen in your heart and mind for those phrases that seem especially pertinent to your life and relationships today. Make a plan for enacting one of those verses today.

Practical Blessing

Bless through time-keeping, part three: Stay late! So many of us bolt from meetings, from church, from encounters. We feel time pressure, and so we miss opportunities to bless. Plan that your time with someone or a group will last several minutes past the official ending time. Use these extra minutes to listen, to care, to bless. Let people know you are not in a hurry to leave them.

....

Week Four

Day 25: Wednesday Morning

Receive the Blessing of God

Comfort, comfort my people, says your God.
Speak tenderly to Jerusalem,
   and cry to her
that her warfare is ended,
   that her iniquity is pardoned,
that she has received from the LORD's hand
   double for all her sins.

A voice cries:
"In the wilderness prepare the way of the LORD;
   make straight in the desert a highway for our God.
Every valley shall be lifted up,
   and every mountain and hill be made low;

the uneven ground shall become level,
   and the rough places a plain.
And the glory of the LORD shall be revealed,
   and all flesh shall see it together,
   for the mouth of the LORD has spoken." . . .

The grass withers, the flower fades,
   but the word of our God will stand forever.
      (Isaiah 40:1-5, 8)

This passage is often read during Advent, the season in which we prepare to celebrate the birth of Christ. What comfort does the prophecy offer us? Can you trust anew that Jesus is the fulfillment of this prophecy? He has come to us once and he will come again. He has secured our forgiveness and eternal life; he will come to fully establish his reign of peace and glory. Pray for his return!

Return the Blessing to God

I will extol you, my God and King,
   and bless your name forever and ever.
Every day I will bless you
   and praise your name forever and ever.
Great is the LORD, and greatly to be praised,
   and his greatness is unsearchable.

One generation shall commend your works to another,
   and shall declare your mighty acts.
On the glorious splendor of your majesty,
   and on your wondrous works, I will meditate.
They shall speak of the might of your awesome deeds,
   and I will declare your greatness.
They shall pour forth the fame of your abundant goodness
   and shall sing aloud of your righteousness.
      (Psalm 145:1-7)

Describe the fame of our triune God of grace. Why should others commend the Lord? Bless the name of the LORD I AM, who is God and king over all.

Reflect the Blessing of God to Others

Then he opened their minds to understand the Scriptures, and said to them, "Thus it is written, that the Christ should suffer and on the third day rise from the dead, and that repentance and forgiveness of sins should be proclaimed in his name to all nations, beginning from Jerusalem. You are witnesses of these things." (Luke 24:45-48)

A witness tells what he has seen and heard. How are you a witness to the truth of Christ's resurrection? What has he done in your life? How is he calling you to bless another by bearing witness to God's goodness and salvation in your life? Today, this very day, will you email, phone, write or go to lunch with someone as a witness to Christ Jesus?

Practical Blessing

Tip well! It chilled me to hear a server say she dreaded Sunday lunch because all the churchgoers demanded so much and tipped so poorly. We can do better. Tip well today. Bless someone even by overtipping.

....

Week Four

Day 26: Thursday Morning

Receive the Blessing of God

I tell you this, brothers: flesh and blood cannot inherit the kingdom of God, nor does the perishable inherit the imperishable. Behold! I tell you a mystery. We shall not all sleep, but we shall all be changed, in a moment, in the twinkling of an eye, at the last trumpet. For the trumpet will sound, and the dead will be raised imperishable, and we shall be changed. For this perishable body must put on the imperishable, and this mortal body must put on immortality. When the perishable puts on the imperishable, and the mortal puts on immortality, then shall come to pass the saying that is written:

> "Death is swallowed up in victory."
> "O death, where is your victory?
>   O death, where is your sting?"

The sting of death is sin, and the power of sin is the law. But thanks be to God, who gives us the victory through our Lord Jesus Christ.

Therefore, my beloved brothers, be steadfast, immovable, always abounding in the work of the Lord, knowing that in the Lord your labor is not in vain. (1 Corinthians 15:50-58)

What is the Christian hope for what happens to us after death? Read this passage as God's voice speaking to the places of grief in your heart. Claim it over loved ones you have lost.

Return the Blessing to God

> Have you not known? Have you not heard?
> The LORD is the everlasting God,
>   the Creator of the ends of the earth.
> He does not faint or grow weary;
>   his understanding is unsearchable.
> He gives power to the faint,
>   and to him who has no might he increases strength.
> Even youths shall faint and be weary,

and young men shall fall exhausted;
but they who wait for the LORD shall renew their streng
they shall mount up with wings like eagles;
they shall run and not be weary;
they shall walk and not faint. (Isaiah 40:28-31)

Bless the Lord by reading this passage aloud several times
your heart to the ancient words as you extol our God and
Draw strength from the Lord's strength.

Reflect the Blessing of God to Others

Give ear, O Shepherd of Israel,
you who lead Joseph like a flock.
You who are enthroned upon the cherubim, shine forth. . . .
Stir up your might
and come to save us!

Restore us, O God;
let your face shine, that we may be saved!

Turn again, O God of hosts!
Look down from heaven, and see. . . .
give us life, and we will call upon your name!

Restore us, O LORD God of hosts!
Let your face shine, that we may be saved! (Psalm 80:1-3,
14, 18-19)

Consider those who feel that God has frowned upon them, who
feel that God is angry with them or punishing them. Pray that the
triune God would shine his face upon their lives so that they might
feel his pleasure. Pray for the restoration of those who are strug-
gling. Consider how you can be the shining face of God in their
lives today.

.actical Blessing

Affirm! People who live the blessing life are positive people. Look for the good in situations and in other people. Draw attention to what is fine, wholesome, delightful. Express your affirmation of others often.

....

Week Four

Day 27: Friday Morning

Receive the Blessing of God

> On this mountain the LORD of hosts will make for all peoples
>   a feast of rich food, a feast of well-aged wine,
>   of rich food full of marrow, of aged wine well refined.
> And he will swallow up on this mountain
>   the covering that is cast over all peoples,
>   the veil that is spread over all nations.
>   He will swallow up death forever;
> and the LORD God will wipe away tears from all faces,
>   and the reproach of his people he will take away from all
>   the earth,
>   for the LORD has spoken.
> It will be said on that day,
>   "Behold, this is our God; we have waited for him, that he
>   might save us.
>   This is the LORD; we have waited for him;
>   let us be glad and rejoice in his salvation." (Isaiah 25:6-9)

In our Friday looks at Old Testament "big vision" passages, we see the universal reach of God's grace. What is promised in this passage? Do you see how Isaiah 25 echoes in the passage we read

Sunday from Revelation 21? In the midst of a world of death, receive the hope God promises.

Return the Blessing to God

> I love the LORD, because he has heard
>> my voice and my pleas for mercy.
> Because he inclined his ear to me,
>> therefore I will call on him as long as I live.
> The snares of death encompassed me;
>> the pangs of Sheol laid hold on me;
>> I suffered distress and anguish.
> Then I called on the name of the LORD:
> "O LORD, I pray, deliver my soul!"
>
> Gracious is the LORD, and righteous;
>> our God is merciful.
> The LORD preserves the simple;
>> when I was brought low, he saved me.
> Return, O my soul, to your rest;
>> for the LORD has dealt bountifully with you. . . .
>
> Precious in the sight of the LORD
>> is the death of his saints. . . .
> I will offer to you the sacrifice of thanksgiving
>> and call on the name of the LORD. (Psalm 116:1-7, 15, 17)

Bless the Lord as you pray this psalm aloud. In particular, bless God as you hold up those who have experienced loss and those whom you have lost to death. Bless God for the deliverance he gives in this life and for the hope he gives us of everlasting life.

Reflect the Blessing of God to Others

> For the grace of God has appeared, bringing salvation for all

people, training us to renounce ungodliness and worldly passions, and to live self-controlled, upright, and godly lives in the present age, waiting for our blessed hope, the appearing of the glory of our great God and Savior Jesus Christ, who gave himself for us to redeem us from all lawlessness and to purify for himself a people for his own possession who are zealous for good works. (Titus 2:11-14)

What are the qualities of the blessing life described in this passage? It contains a rhythm of turning away from some things and turning positively to enact others. What are you called to renounce today? What you are called to do? What good work are you called to offer as a blessing to others today?

Practical Blessing

Move some treasure! One of the best ways to enter the flow of God's blessing life is to pass along a portion of the bounty he gives us. Today, write a check to a ministry or person you desire to support. Do it now!

....

Week Four

Day 28: Saturday Morning

Receive the Blessing of God

So then, brothers, we are debtors, not to the flesh, to live according to the flesh. For if you live according to the flesh you will die, but if by the Spirit you put to death the deeds of the body, you will live. For all who are led by the Spirit of God are sons of God. For you did not receive the spirit of slavery to fall back into fear, but you have received the Spirit of adoption as sons, by whom we cry, "Abba! Father!" The Spirit himself bears witness with our spirit that we are children of God, and if children, then heirs—heirs of God and fellow heirs with Christ, provided we suffer with him in order that we may also be glorified with him. (Romans 8:12-17)

In this passage, what blessings does the Spirit give us? Can you feel the blessed Spirit crying out to the Father through you? Speak aloud those words, "Abba, Father." Extend your hands to your heavenly Father. Visualize him picking you up and holding you in love.

Return the Blessing to God

Have this mind among yourselves, which is yours in Christ Jesus, who, though he was in the form of God, did not count equality with God a thing to be grasped, but emptied himself, by taking the form of a servant, being born in the likeness of men. And being found in human form, he humbled himself by becoming obedient to the point of death, even death on a cross. Therefore God has highly exalted him and bestowed on him the name that is above every name, so that at the name of Jesus every knee should bow, in heaven and on earth and under the earth, and every tongue confess that Jesus Christ is Lord, to the glory of God the Father. (Philippians 2:5-11)

This is one of the earliest and greatest hymns to Jesus. Consider all the Christians through the centuries to whom you are linked as you bless Jesus by praying aloud these words. Do it more than once.

Reflect the Blessing of God to Others

Therefore, my beloved, as you have always obeyed, so now, not only as in my presence but much more in my absence, work out your own salvation with fear and trembling, for it is God who works in you, both to will and to work for his good pleasure.

Do all things without grumbling or disputing, that you may be blameless and innocent, children of God without blemish in the midst of a crooked and twisted generation, among whom you shine as lights in the world, holding fast to the word of life, so that in the day of Christ I may be proud that I did not run in vain or labor in vain. (Philippians 2:12-16)

Weekend Stretch

God works in us to save us and change us. But we also work. We work out moment by moment the implications of all he has done for us in Jesus. In what ways does this passage describe how we are to be blessing the world?

The Greek phrase translated as "holding fast to the word of life" can also be translated as "holding forth the word of life." How are both holding fast and holding forth necessary for us?

Consider how Paul recognizes that the world is "crooked and twisted." But notice that he does not send us to condemn the world or leave the world. We are sent to shine light and offer the word of life. In other words, we are sent to bless!

How do you intentionally shine God's light in this world—at your work, in your neighborhood? Can you identify a specific ministry to the needy in which you are involved? If not, pick one today.

....

Week Five

Day 29: Sunday Morning

Receive the Blessing of God

But we do not want you to be uninformed, brothers, about

those who are asleep, that you may not grieve as others do who have no hope. For since we believe that Jesus died and rose again, even so, through Jesus, God will bring with him those who have fallen asleep. For this we declare to you by a word from the Lord, that we who are alive, who are left until the coming of the Lord, will not precede those who have fallen asleep. For the Lord himself will descend from heaven with a cry of command, with the voice of an archangel, and with the sound of the trumpet of God. And the dead in Christ will rise first. Then we who are alive, who are left, will be caught up together with them in the clouds to meet the Lord in the air, and so we will always be with the Lord. (1 Thessalonians 4:13-17)

The Christian hope is that we will be together with the Lord and with one another. As you consider loved ones you have lost, receive this promise of seeing them again. Consider that the story of Jesus is not over: he is going to return. Apply this news to difficult or even hopeless situations you encounter in this world.

Return the Blessing to God

Make a joyful noise to the LORD, all the earth!
  Serve the LORD with gladness!
  Come into his presence with singing!

Know that the LORD, he is God!
  It is he who made us, and we are his;
  we are his people, and the sheep of his pasture.

Enter his gates with thanksgiving,
  and his courts with praise!
  Give thanks to him; bless his name!

For the LORD is good;
> his steadfast love endures forever,
> and his faithfulness to all generations. (Psalm 100)

Bless God for the fact that you belong to him. As the old prayer affirms, you are a sheep of his own fold, a sinner of his own redeeming, a child of his own heart. Sing to the Lord the joy of belonging to him. Tell him today how you know that his steadfast love endures forever. Do your best to make merry before the triune God who made you, redeemed you and will never leave you.

Reflect the Blessing of God to Others

> I therefore, a prisoner for the Lord, urge you to walk in a manner worthy of the calling to which you have been called with all humility and gentleness, with patience, bearing with one another in love, eager to maintain the unity of the Spirit in the bond of peace. (Ephesians 4:1-3)

Our calling to eternal life is great. So our walk, our way of living, should reflect this grace and hope. In particular, with whom might you be called to show patience today? Can you plan now to bear with a difficult person in view of how the Lord has been so kind to you? What is a way you can strengthen peace and unity among the believers in your sphere of influence?

Practical Blessing

Practice gentleness! It's all too easy to be abrupt or rough, especially with the people we love the most. All the fruits of the Spirit bless others. As we cultivate gentleness, people will be able to trust us, to relax around us, to share with us. Bless someone with gentleness today.

....

Week Five

Day 30: Monday Morning

Receive the Blessing of God

> But as he considered these things, behold, an angel of the Lord appeared to him in a dream, saying, "Joseph, son of David, do not fear to take Mary as your wife, for that which is conceived in her is from the Holy Spirit. She will bear a son, and you shall call his name Jesus, for he will save his people from their sins." All this took place to fulfill what the Lord had spoken by the prophet:
>
> > "Behold, the virgin shall conceive and bear a son,
> >   and they shall call his name Immanuel"
>
> (which means, God with us). (Matthew 1:20-23)

Matthew tells the Christmas story from Joseph's point of view. He had to receive the news of Christ in spite of his doubts about Mary and the baby's conception. Sometimes we, too, fear to embrace the wondrous news of Immanuel, God with us. Will you summon the courage today to make an act of faith whereby you receive Jesus, whose name means the LORD saves, who has indeed come to save you from your sins?

Return the Blessing to God

> I will bless the LORD at all times;
>   his praise shall continually be in my mouth.
> My soul makes its boast in the LORD;
>   let the humble hear and be glad.

Oh, magnify the LORD with me,
  and let us exalt his name together!

I sought the LORD, and he answered me
  and delivered me from all my fears.
Those who look to him are radiant,
  and their faces shall never be ashamed.
This poor man cried, and the LORD heard him
  and saved him out of all his troubles.
The angel of the LORD encamps
  around those who fear him, and delivers them.

Oh, taste and see that the LORD is good!
  Blessed is the man who takes refuge in him!
Oh, fear the LORD, you his saints,
  for those who fear him have no lack!
The young lions suffer want and hunger;
  but those who seek the LORD lack no good thing. (Psalm
    34:1-10)

David put the praise of God in his mouth. Get the blessing of the triune God of grace going on your tongue this morning. Let your lips form words of praise. Praise God for the times when you were "this poor man" and cried out to him, then found that God answered and saved you. Let the goodness of the Lord be a taste of life you savor all day long.

Reflect the Blessing of God to Others

Come, O children, listen to me;
  I will teach you the fear of the LORD.
What man is there who desires life
  and loves many days, that he may see good?
Keep your tongue from evil

and your lips from speaking deceit.
Turn away from evil and do good;
    seek peace and pursue it. (Psalm 34:11-14)

Psalm 34 turns from praise to considering how we are to live in view of God's steadfast love and mercy. According to this psalm, what is the secret to finding a life we love? Note how one way to keep from saying ugly things is to keep the praise of God on your lips. What harsh habits of speech will you turn from today? With whom do you need to "seek peace and pursue it"? What specifically will you do this very day to show you are pursuing that peace?

Practical Blessing

Make peace! Harmony is a great blessing, but it takes work. It takes humility. Is there a relationship in which you need to swallow your pride and make the first move? Do you need to say, "I'm sorry"? Can you be the one to cross the divide and seek peace today?

....

Week Five

Day 31: Tuesday Morning

Receive the Blessing of God

Jesus said to her, "I am the resurrection and the life. Whoever believes in me, though he die, yet shall he live, and everyone who lives and believes in me shall never die. Do you believe this?" She said to him, "Yes, Lord; I believe that you are the Christ, the Son of God, who is coming into the world." (John 11:25-27)

Tuesday brings reflection on Jesus' statements about himself in John. In this passage Jesus is speaking to Martha, whose brother Lazarus has recently died. He promises her that he is the resurrection and the life. He has life in himself. He is the source of all life and he will bring to life again those who die belonging to him. He gives us this eternal life to experience now through his Holy Spirit. These are huge claims! So he asked Martha, "Do you believe this?" He asks each of us to receive the blessing of his life as he asks us, "Will you believe that I am the resurrection this very day?"

Return the Blessing to God

The LORD is my shepherd; I shall not want.

He maketh me to lie down in green pastures: he leadeth me beside the still waters.

He restoreth my soul: he leadeth me in the paths of righteousness for his name's sake.

Yea, though I walk through the valley of the shadow of death, I will fear no evil: for thou art with me; thy rod and thy staff they comfort me.

Thou preparest a table before me in the presence of mine enemies: thou anointest my head with oil; my cup runneth over.

Surely goodness and mercy shall follow me all the days of my life: and I will dwell in the house of the LORD for ever. (Psalm 23 KJV)

Resurrection follows death. But we also know how God saves us from death, both literal and spiritual, in this world. Recall when you have walked through the valley of the shadow of death. How did the Lord deliver you? How does he sustain you now in the "land of the living"? Bless him for the life he gives you this moment and in each situation.

Reflect the Blessing of God to Others

> What shall I render to the LORD
> for all his benefits to me?
> I will lift up the cup of salvation
> and call on the name of the LORD,
> I will pay my vows to the LORD
> in the presence of all his people. . . .
>
> Praise the LORD! (Psalm 116:12-13, 19)

When we have known deliverance from death and sustaining life even in the midst of loss, we desire to make a return of thanks to the Lord of life. This psalm tells us that we bless the Lord as we worship (lifting the cup of salvation and calling on him) and obey him (paying our vows). Living a life of thanks and faithfulness openly before others blesses them. Jesus urged us to let our light shine before others. How could you be more intentional in your words and acts today to show others that you belong to the God of grace and glory?

Practical Blessing

Praise in the midday! We often get so busy in a day that we forget to pause to bless God. Schedule a time right now for ten minutes during today when you can lift your heart and voice to God in blessing.

. . . .

Week Five

Day 32: Wednesday Morning

Receive the Blessing of God

> But now thus says the LORD,
> he who created you, O Jacob,

he who formed you, O Israel:
"Fear not, for I have redeemed you;
   I have called you by name, you are mine.
When you pass through the waters, I will be with you;
   and through the rivers, they shall not overwhelm you;
when you walk through fire you shall not be burned,
   and the flame shall not consume you.
For I am the LORD your God,
   the Holy One of Israel, your Savior. . . .
You are precious in my eyes,
   and honored, and I love you. . . .
Fear not, for I am with you." (Isaiah 43:1-5)

Wednesday means another great passage from Isaiah: Hear these words spoken to you: "You are precious in my eyes, and honored, and I love you." Receive the truth of the Father's love for you, his beloved child. Don't squirm from his arms or doubt his loving words. Imagine what your day would be like if all day long you were aware that "I am precious to God."

Return the Blessing to God

The LORD is gracious and merciful,
   slow to anger and abounding in steadfast love.
The LORD is good to all,
   and his mercy is over all that he has made.

All your works shall give thanks to you, O LORD,
   and all your saints shall bless you!
They shall speak of the glory of your kingdom
   and tell of your power,
to make known to the children of man your mighty deeds,
   and the glorious splendor of your kingdom.

Your kingdom is an everlasting kingdom,
>   and your dominion endures throughout all generations.

The LORD is faithful in all his words
>   and kind in all his works.
The LORD upholds all who are falling
>   and raises up all who are bowed down.
The eyes of all look to you,
>   and you give them their food in due season.
You open your hand;
>   you satisfy the desire of every living thing.
The LORD is righteous in all his ways
>   and kind in all his works.
The LORD is near to all who call on him,
>   to all who call on him in truth.
He fulfills the desire of those who fear him;
>   he also hears their cry and saves them.
The LORD preserves all who love him,
>   but all the wicked he will destroy.

My mouth will speak the praise of the LORD,
>   and let all flesh bless his holy name forever and ever.
>   (Psalm 145:8-21)

Bless the God who knows you by name by speaking well of his name. Use this psalm to describe our great God and all he does for us. Say it or sing it aloud at least twice. Expand in your own words on phrases that move you.

Reflect the Blessing of God to Others

"As you sent me into the world, so I have sent them into the world. . . .

"I do not ask for these only, but also for those who will

believe in me through their word, that they may all be one, just as you, Father, are in me, and I in you, that they also may be in us, so that the world may believe that you have sent me." (John 17:18-21)

God has chosen to reach those who do not know him through those who do know him now. He blesses us so that we may bless others. In particular, he desires the world to know Jesus, and so he sends us into the world with his gospel. When did you last tell someone about your blessing God? To whom might he be sending you to speak of Jesus even today?

Practical Blessing

Be faithful. This fruit of the Spirit blesses others as we keep faith with them. Others are blessed as they find us reliable, with a word that can be trusted. Others are blessed as we do what we promise and enact what is rightfully expected of us. Show up as a faithful one today.

....

Week Five

Day 33: Thursday Morning

Receive the Blessing of God

Therefore, if anyone is in Christ, he is a new creation. The old has passed away; behold, the new has come. All this is from God, who through Christ reconciled us to himself and gave us the ministry of reconciliation; that is, in Christ God was reconciling the world to himself, not counting their trespasses against them, and entrusting to us the message of reconciliation. Therefore, we are ambassadors for Christ, God making his appeal through us. We implore you on behalf of Christ, be reconciled to God. For our sake he made him to be sin who knew no sin, so that in him we might become the righteousness of God. (2 Corinthians 5:17-21)

Our God is intent on getting reunited to us. Christ actually became sin so that we might become the righteousness of God. That's mystical! He swaps us: his purity for our filthiness, his goodness for our evil, his peace for our anxiety, his forgiveness for our guilt. When we say "yes" to this cosmic trade, we actually get remade. We become a new creation—still us but with God's Spirit living within us. Will you say "yes" afresh to this reconciliation with God today?

Return the Blessing to God

Praise the LORD!
I will give thanks to the LORD with my whole heart,
    in the company of the upright, in the congregation.
Great are the works of the LORD,
    studied by all who delight in them.
Full of splendor and majesty is his work,
    and his righteousness endures forever.
He has caused his wondrous works to be remembered;
    the LORD is gracious and merciful.
He provides food for those who fear him;
    he remembers his covenant forever.
He has shown his people the power of his works,
    in giving them the inheritance of the nations.
The works of his hands are faithful and just;
    all his precepts are trustworthy;
they are established forever and ever,
    to be performed with faithfulness and uprightness.

He sent redemption to his people;
> he has commanded his covenant forever.
Holy and awesome is his name!
The fear of the LORD is the beginning of wisdom;
> all those who practice it have a good understanding.
His praise endures forever! (Psalm 111)

As you pray this psalm aloud, hold in your mind the truth that the mightiest of the mighty works of God is the reconciliation he has created for us in Christ Jesus. Bless him for the mystery and majesty of the redemption he has sent us. Lift up the wisdom of his plan and extol the greatness of his faithfulness.

Reflect the Blessing of God to Others

> God . . . gave us the ministry of reconciliation; that is, in Christ God was reconciling the world to himself, not counting their trespasses against them, and entrusting to us the message of reconciliation. Therefore, we are ambassadors for Christ, God making his appeal through us. We implore you on behalf of Christ, be reconciled to God. (2 Corinthians 5:18-20)

Paul understood that God's chosen way of spreading the news of his love is person to person. We who know Jesus are now ambassadors for him—each and every one of us. We all have a part in the ministry of reconciliation. That's the massive blessing project of the triune God—to urge everyone to make peace with him, because he has made peace with us through Christ. To whom are you sent today? If there was one person you knew God was sending you to, who would that be? How will you contact that person today? How will you express the message of Christ's reconciliation? If not you, then who will go?

Practical Blessing

Love! We have implied this all along, but let's just say it. Blessing means loving. Our blessing God is love. We show his love as we love others. Love well your loved ones today! Love beyond your loved ones in the name of your blessing Father through Jesus, God's blessing in the flesh, by the power of the blessed Spirit.

Week Five

Day 34: Friday Morning

Receive the Blessing of God

> Then I saw a new heaven and a new earth, for the first heaven and the first earth had passed away, and the sea was no more. And I saw the holy city, new Jerusalem, coming down out of heaven from God, prepared as a bride adorned for her husband. And I heard a loud voice from the throne saying, "Behold, the dwelling place of God is with man. He will dwell with them, and they will be his people, and God himself will be with them as their God. He will wipe away every tear from their eyes, and death shall be no more, neither shall there be mourning, nor crying, nor pain anymore, for the former things have passed away."
>
> And he who was seated on the throne said, "Behold, I am making all things new." Also he said, "Write this down, for these words are trustworthy and true." And he said to me, "It is done! I am the Alpha and the Omega, the beginning and the end. To the thirsty I will give from the spring of the water of life without payment." (Revelation 21:1-6)

Our Friday passages celebrate the covenant promise of God

woven through the pages of Scripture: I will be their God and they
will be my people. Can you catch the triune God's vision for the
new heaven and the new earth in this passage? Which parts especially draw your attention today? Carry the truth of this vision
with you into the world.

Return the Blessing to God

I charge you in the presence of God, who gives life to all
things, and of Christ Jesus, who in his testimony before
Pontius Pilate made the good confession, to keep the com-
mandment unstained and free from reproach until the appearing of our Lord Jesus Christ, which he will display at the
proper time—he who is the blessed and only Sovereign, the
King of kings and Lord of lords, who alone has immortality,
who dwells in unapproachable light, whom no one has ever
seen or can see. To him be honor and eternal dominion.
Amen. (1 Timothy 6:13-16)

While Paul was writing to encourage Timothy, he just broke into
song! As he contemplated the return of Jesus, he thrilled to the truth
and praised Christ. Bless Jesus today through the words of verses 15
and 16. It's okay if you hum Handel's Hallelujah Chorus as you do!

Reflect the Blessing of God to Others

As for the rich in this present age, charge them not to be
haughty, nor to set their hopes on the uncertainty of riches,
but on God, who richly provides us with everything to enjoy.
They are to do good, to be rich in good works, to be generous
and ready to share, thus storing up treasure for themselves as
a good foundation for the future, so that they may take hold
of that which is truly life. (1 Timothy 6:17-19)

What's the purpose of having been richly provided for in this world? How might you be called to share some of your material provision today? How might you use money to do good to someone today?

Practical Blessing

Open your wallet! Can you prepare yourself to be openhanded and generous with others as a way to bless them? Might you take someone to lunch? Put a quarter in an expired parking meter? Pick up the tab on the order of the person behind you in the line? Drop a gift at the local sharing center?

....

Week Five

Day 35: Saturday Morning

Receive the Blessing of God

> For I consider that the sufferings of this present time are not worth comparing with the glory that is to be revealed to us. For the creation waits with eager longing for the revealing of the sons of God. For the creation was subjected to futility, not willingly, but because of him who subjected it, in hope that the creation itself will be set free from its bondage to corruption and obtain the freedom of the glory of the children of God. For we know that the whole creation has been groaning together in the pains of childbirth until now. And not only the creation, but we ourselves, who have the firstfruits of the Spirit, groan inwardly as we wait eagerly for adoption as sons, the redemption of our bodies. For in this hope we were saved. Now hope that is seen is not hope. For who hopes for what

he sees? But if we hope for what we do not see, we wait for it with patience. (Romans 8:18-25)

Romans 8 goes right to the very heart of God and his purposes for us. Notice how Christ's salvation is not just about us but about the whole creation. Hold this vision up to the ways you see decay and futility today. Be hopeful! Hope God's vision into the world today. Fan hope into flame as you lean on the truth of these promises.

Return the Blessing to God

This is the day that the LORD has made;
let us rejoice and be glad in it.
Save us, we pray, O LORD!
O LORD, we pray, give us success!
Blessed is he who comes in the name of the LORD!
We bless you from the house of the LORD.
The LORD is God,
and he has made his light to shine upon us.
Bind the festal sacrifice with cords,
up to the horns of the altar!
You are my God, and I will give thanks to you;
you are my God; I will extol you.
Oh give thanks to the LORD, for he is good;
for his steadfast love endures forever! (Psalm 118:24-29)

This psalm calls us to rejoice in the gift of this particular day. Be glad before the Lord. Shed anxious thoughts. Reject feelings of disappointment about the state of your life. Deny dissatisfaction a place in your day. Bless God for this hour that you are alive and claim him, cling to him as you say, "You are my God!"

Reflect the Blessing of God to Others

Therefore, having put away falsehood, let each one of you speak the truth with his neighbor, for we are members one of another. Be angry and do not sin; do not let the sun go down on your anger, and give no opportunity to the devil. Let the thief no longer steal, but rather let him labor, doing honest work with his own hands, so that he may have something to share with anyone in need. Let no corrupting talk come out of your mouths, but only such as is good for building up, as fits the occasion, that it may give grace to those who hear. And do not grieve the Holy Spirit of God, by whom you were sealed for the day of redemption. Let all bitterness and wrath and anger and clamor and slander be put away from you, along with all malice. Be kind to one another, tenderhearted, forgiving one another, as God in Christ forgave you. (Ephesians 4:25-32)

Weekend Blessing

The people who rejoice that God is already pleased with us in Christ now live to please God in gratitude. This passage lists a number of concrete ways to bless others: by sharing, by our speech that builds up, by kindness and forgiveness. Write a blessing plan for this weekend. In other words, write down the area in which you feel particularly called to work today. Describe how you will build up someone with your words. Or describe in what way you will show kindness to someone. Or write down who and what you need to forgive and plan to do that today.

Week Six

Day 36: Sunday Morning

Receive the Blessing of God

What then shall we say to these things? If God is for us, who can be against us? He who did not spare his own Son but gave him up for us all, how will he not also with him graciously give us all things? Who shall bring any charge against God's elect? It is God who justifies. Who is to condemn? Christ Jesus is the one who died—more than that, who was raised—who is at the right hand of God, who indeed is interceding for us. Who shall separate us from the love of Christ? Shall tribulation, or distress, or persecution, or famine, or nakedness, or danger, or sword? As it is written,

> "For your sake we are being killed all the day long;
> we are regarded as sheep to be slaughtered."

No, in all these things we are more than conquerors through him who loved us. For I am sure that neither death nor life, nor angels nor rulers, nor things present nor things to come, nor powers, nor height nor depth, nor anything else in all creation, will be able to separate us from the love of God in Christ Jesus our Lord. (Romans 8:31-39)

Nothing can separate us from the love of God! Therefore all things, even the worst things, can be used by God for our greater good and his glory. Consider the voices that try to tell you that you can be cut off from God's love—voices of doubt, accusation, circumstance, despair. Read them back the affirmation of this passage which begins, "No, in all these things . . ." Claim the love of God in Christ Jesus!

Return the Blessing to God

The LORD is merciful and gracious,
>   slow to anger and abounding in steadfast love.
He will not always chide,
>   nor will he keep his anger forever.
He does not deal with us according to our sins,
>   nor repay us according to our iniquities.
For as high as the heavens are above the earth,
>   so great is his steadfast love toward those who fear him;
as far as the east is from the west,
>   so far does he remove our transgressions from us.
As a father shows compassion to his children,
>   so the LORD shows compassion to those who fear him.
For he knows our frame;
>   he remembers that we are dust.
As for man, his days are like grass;
>   he flourishes like a flower of the field;
for the wind passes over it, and it is gone,
>   and its place knows it no more.
But the steadfast love of the LORD is from everlasting to
>   everlasting on those who fear him,
>   and his righteousness to children's children,
to those who keep his covenant
>   and remember to do his commandments. (Psalm
>   103:8-18)

Bless God for his promises in Romans 8 by using part of the majestic Psalm 103. Notice how the passages relate to one another as you praise the triune God who has forgiven you and given you his steadfast, unbreakable love.

Reflect the Blessing of God to Others

> To this end we always pray for you, that our God may make you worthy of his calling and may fulfill every resolve for good and every work of faith by his power, so that the name of our Lord Jesus may be glorified in you, and you in him, according to the grace of our God and the Lord Jesus Christ. (2 Thessalonians 1:11-12)

> Now may our Lord Jesus Christ himself, and God our Father, who loved us and gave us eternal comfort and good hope through grace, comfort your hearts and establish them in every good work and word. (2 Thessalonians 2:16-17)

The calling of God to this unbreakable love is more than we can ever deserve. Yet we can carry ourselves as those who have accepted this gift. We can conduct ourselves in the Spirit's power according to our station in the universe: ransomed, freed, restored, forgiven. In that power, what good works for others do you resolve to do this day? Who needs a touch of the comfort you have already known in Christ? What work of faith beckons you?

Practical Blessing

Speak a word! In our final week, it may now be time to go on and give a biblical blessing to someone. Perhaps a child or grandchild or grandmother or friend in the hospital—the Lord will lead you. But write down one of these great benedictions, or mark one of the psalms you have read, and speak it over someone when the time is right, with your hand on their shoulder or head. Ask, "May I bless you?" And then do it!

....

Week Six

Day 37: Monday Morning

Receive the Blessing of God

In the beginning was the Word, and the Word was with God, and the Word was God. He was in the beginning with God. All things were made through him, and without him was not any thing made that was made. In him was life, and the life was the light of men. The light shines in the darkness, and the darkness has not overcome it.

There was a man sent from God, whose name was John. He came as a witness, to bear witness about the light, that all might believe through him. He was not the light, but came to bear witness about the light.

The true light, which gives light to everyone, was coming into the world. He was in the world, and the world was made through him, yet the world did not know him. He came to his own, and his own people did not receive him. But to all who did receive him, who believed in his name, he gave the right to become children of God, who were born, not of blood nor of the will of the flesh nor of the will of man, but of God.

And the Word became flesh and dwelt among us, and we have seen his glory, glory as of the only Son from the Father, full of grace and truth. . . . For from his fullness we have all received, grace upon grace. For the law was given through Moses; grace and truth came through Jesus Christ. No one has ever seen God; the only God, who is at the Father's side, he has made him known. (John 1:1-18)

We've been looking on Mondays at how Jesus entered the world. John's unique view reminds us that the Word became flesh. The Word is the eternal Son of God through whom all things were created. The unseen God showed his face in Jesus Christ. God came to us! Can you receive the blessing that God loves us so much that he did not remain aloof or apart from us but actually came to us in the flesh? Can you receive the light that shines even in the deepest darkness? Can you believe the promise that those who so receive him actually become children of God?

Return the Blessing to God

And after you have suffered a little while, the God of all grace, who has called you to his eternal glory in Christ, will himself restore, confirm, strengthen, and establish you. To him be the dominion forever and ever. Amen. (1 Peter 5:10-11)

We have all walked in darkness, far from the light. We have all known the oppression of this world and the weariness of life in it. Many are acutely suffering even now. But God has not forgotten us. Give thanks to him as you pray back the promise that he will restore you. Bless him for the call to eternal glory which follows this brief life in this difficult world. Affirm to the triune God of grace that you know he has the dominion even over what you face in life today.

Reflect the Blessing of God to Others

And we urge you, brothers, admonish the idle, encourage the fainthearted, help the weak, be patient with them all. See that no one repays anyone evil for evil, but always seek to do good to one another and to everyone. Rejoice always, pray without ceasing, give thanks in all circumstances; for this is the will of

God in Christ Jesus for you. Do not quench the Spirit. Do not despise prophecies, but test everything; hold fast what is good. Abstain from every form of evil.

Now may the God of peace himself sanctify you completely, and may your whole spirit and soul and body be kept blameless at the coming of our Lord Jesus Christ. He who calls you is faithful; he will surely do it. (1 Thessalonians 5:14-24)

Blessing others can include admonishment—letting someone know they are called to more—as well as encouragement. But this is to be done in patience and gentleness. Is there a difficult word you have been called to give as a way of blessing another?

Practical Blessing

Know peace! Our embracing of the blessing life has led us to see that our sovereign God is engaged in a massive blessing project for his lost world. This can give us deep peace even in the midst of strife. Don't let surface waves prevent you from realizing the deep ocean of peace you have in Christ. Be a person who is grounded in the peace that passes understanding. Avoid common panics and stay grounded—it will bless others.

....

Week Six

Day 38: Tuesday Morning

Receive the Blessing of God

"I am the true vine, and my Father is the vinedresser. Every branch in me that does not bear fruit he takes away, and every branch that does bear fruit he prunes, that it may bear more fruit. Already you are clean because of the word that I have spoken to you. Abide in me, and I in you. As the branch cannot bear fruit by itself, unless it abides in the vine, neither can you, unless you abide in me. I am the vine; you are the branches. Whoever abides in me and I in him, he it is that bears much fruit, for apart from me you can do nothing." (John 15:1-5)

In the Old Testament, Israel was described as the Lord's vine. But God's people could not bring forth the fruit of faithfulness that our God requires. Jesus came to do for us what we could not do ourselves. Now, connected to his faithfulness and the power of his life, we draw upon him in faith to live in love and worship. Today, leave off trying to live apart from him. Instead, live from Jesus as you receive the blessing that he is the vine, the true source of life.

Return the Blessing to God

If it had not been the LORD who was on our side—
    let Israel now say—
if it had not been the LORD who was on our side
    when people rose up against us,
then they would have swallowed us up alive,
    when their anger was kindled against us;
then the flood would have swept us away,
    the torrent would have gone over us;
then over us would have gone
    the raging waters.

Blessed be the LORD,
    who has not given us
    as prey to their teeth!
We have escaped like a bird
    from the snare of the fowlers;

the snare is broken,
  and we have escaped!

Our help is in the name of the LORD,
  who made heaven and earth. (Psalm 124)

As you bless the Lord today, recall that apart from him we can do nothing. Without the Lord, we would never have made it! Bless the Lord who delivers us as you pray this psalm aloud.

Reflect the Blessing of God to Others

Continue steadfastly in prayer, being watchful in it with thanksgiving. At the same time, pray also for us, that God may open to us a door for the word, to declare the mystery of Christ, on account of which I am in prison—that I may make it clear, which is how I ought to speak.

Walk in wisdom toward outsiders, making the best use of the time. Let your speech always be gracious, seasoned with salt, so that you may know how you ought to answer each person. (Colossians 4:2-6)

Who comes to mind today as in particular need of encouraging prayer? Pray for those people. Pray as well for people you know in direct mission work, that doors would open for them. Give them the blessing of your prayer energy today. Then consider that you can also give gracious speech by letting people know you prayed for them today.

Practical Blessing

Pray! Go through your day realizing that prayer is a mighty instrument of blessing. Look, listen and pray. That is, see how it is with someone, listen for a need, and then shoot God a short sentence prayer asking for his blessing in their life. Cultivate a habit of making short blessing prayers throughout the day.

Week Six

Day 39: Wednesday Morning

Receive the Blessing of God

> "Come, everyone who thirsts,
>   come to the waters;
> and he who has no money,
>   come, buy and eat!
> Come, buy wine and milk
>   without money and without price.
> Why do you spend your money for that which is not bread,
>   and your labor for that which does not satisfy?
> Listen diligently to me, and eat what is good,
>   and delight yourselves in rich food.
> Incline your ear, and come to me;
>   hear, that your soul may live;
> and I will make with you an everlasting covenant,
>   my steadfast, sure love for David." (Isaiah 55:1-3)

We've all spent energy on what does not bring life. We've worked for what does not satisfy. We've tried to buy life that only God can give. Today, hear the gracious invitation of our God to come to him as to the source of all good and fulfillment. Come with nothing to offer but a receptive spirit to what God offers.

Return the Blessing to God

> Praise the LORD!
> Praise God in his sanctuary;
>   praise him in his mighty heavens!

Praise him for his mighty deeds;
    praise him according to his excellent greatness!

Praise him with trumpet sound;
    praise him with lute and harp!
Praise him with tambourine and dance;
    praise him with strings and pipe
Praise him with sounding cymbals;
    praise him with loud clashing cymbals!
Let everything that has breath praise the LORD!
Praise the LORD! (Psalm 150)

The final psalm calls for God to be blessed with every instrument in every place among all creatures. This morning find a place to clap, tap, beat and shout praise to God. I'm serious! Find a way to make some noise in honor of God.

Reflect the Blessing of God to Others

Now to him who is able to strengthen you according to my gospel and the preaching of Jesus Christ, according to the revelation of the mystery that was kept secret for long ages but has now been disclosed and through the prophetic writings has been made known to all nations, according to the command of the eternal God, to bring about the obedience of faith—to the only wise God be glory forevermore through Jesus Christ! Amen. (Romans 16:25-27)

Who do you know who needs strengthening today? Who needs strength in particular for "the obedience of faith"? Pray gospel strength for them today. Consider how you will communicate this prayer to them—by phone, email, card, text or visit.

Practical Blessing

Know joy! Those who live the blessing life are people of joy. Our joy is anchored not in circumstances but in the salvation and victory of Jesus. As we have cultivated the habit of blessing God through his Word, we tap into the source of joy. Today, let it out! Go into your world with the joy of your God flowing from within. Claim it. Live it. Show it.

....

Week Six

Day 40: Thursday Morning

Receive the Blessing of God

> Then the angel showed me the river of the water of life, bright as crystal, flowing from the throne of God and of the Lamb through the middle of the street of the city; also, on either side of the river, the tree of life with its twelve kinds of fruit, yielding its fruit each month. The leaves of the tree were for the healing of the nations. No longer will there be anything accursed, but the throne of God and of the Lamb will be in it, and his servants will worship him. They will see his face, and his name will be on their foreheads. (Revelation 22:1-4)

This is the final vision in Scripture. The triune God of grace has a plan for restoring all things in the new heavens and the new earth. Will you trust the hope of what God has promised to do? Will you live from that faith today?

Return the Blessing to God

> John to the seven churches that are in Asia:

Grace to you and peace from him who is and who was and who is to come, and from the seven spirits who are before his throne, and from Jesus Christ the faithful witness, the firstborn of the dead, and the ruler of kings on earth.

To him who loves us and has freed us from our sins by his blood and made us a kingdom, priests to his God and Father, to him be glory and dominion forever and ever. Amen. Behold, he is coming with the clouds, and every eye will see him, even those who pierced him, and all tribes of the earth will wail on account of him. Even so. Amen.

"I am the Alpha and the Omega," says the Lord God, "who is and who was and who is to come, the Almighty." (Revelation 1:4-8)

"Fear not, I am the first and the last, and the living one. I died, and behold I am alive forevermore, and I have the keys of Death and Hades." (Revelation 1:17-18)

Bless Jesus for being the Alpha and the Omega, the first and the last. Tell him you know he's got the whole world in his hands. Tell him you know he's got all of time and history in his hands. Tell him that though there are many rulers in the world, he is the true king.

Reflect the Blessing of God to Others

Put on then, as God's chosen ones, holy and beloved, compassionate hearts, kindness, humility, meekness, and patience, bearing with one another and, if one has a complaint against another, forgiving each other; as the Lord has forgiven you, so you also must forgive. And above all these put on love, which binds everything together in perfect harmony. And let the peace of Christ rule in your hearts, to which indeed you were called in one body. And be thankful. Let the word of Christ dwell in you richly, teaching and admonishing one another in all wisdom, singing psalms and hymns and spiritual songs, with thankfulness in your hearts to God. And whatever you do, in word or deed, do everything in the name of the Lord Jesus, giving thanks to God the Father through him. (Colossians 3:12-17)

Practical Blessing

You've made it! Forty days of intentionally living the blessing life. This final passage sums up the essence of the blessing life: whatever you do, in word or deed, do everything in the name of the Lord Jesus, giving thanks to God the Father through him. Living aware of all Jesus has done. Giving thanks as routinely as breathing. Doing all we do—at work, home or school—as for the Lord, knowing that how we bless others is how we bless him. Go forth and bless!

Download a free
small group leader's guide
for this book at
www.ivpress.com.

Also Available:

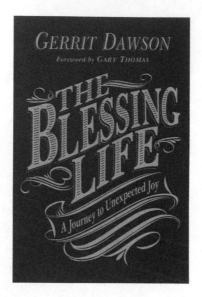

The Blessing Life: A Journey to Unexpected Joy
By Gerrit Dawson